CW00552376

RAILROAD NOIR

RAILROADS PAST AND PRESENT

George M. Smerk, editor

RAILROAD NOIR

THE AMERICAN WEST
at the End of the Twentieth Century

Narratives by LINDA GRANT NIEMANN

Photographs by JOEL JENSEN

Indiana University Press

Bloomington & Indianapolis

This book is a publication of

Indiana University Press
601 North Morton Street
Bloomington, Indiana 47404-3797 USA

www.iupress.indiana.edu

Telephone orders   800-842-6796
Fax orders   812-855-7931
Orders by e-mail   iuporder@indiana.edu

© 2010 by Linda Niemann and Joel Jensen
All rights reserved

No part of this book may be reproduced or utilized in any form
or by any means, electronic or mechanical, including photocopy-
ing and recording, or by any information storage and retrieval
system, without permission in writing from the publisher. The
Association of American University Presses' Resolution on
Permissions constitutes the only exception to this prohibition.

∞ The paper used in this publication meets the minimum requirements of the American National Standard
for Information Sciences—Permanence of Paper for
Printed Library Materials, ANSI Z39.48-1992.

Printed in China

Library of Congress Cataloging-in-Publication Data

Niemann, Linda.
  Railroad noir : the American West at the end of
the twentieth century / narratives by Linda Grant
Niemann ; photographs by Joel Jensen.
    p. cm. — (Railroads past and present)
  ISBN 978-0-253-35446-4 (cl : alk. paper) 1. Railroads—
West (U.S.)—Employees—History. 2. Railroads—Social
aspects—West (U.S.)—History. I. Jensen, Joel. II. Title.
  HD8039.R12U659 2010
  385.092—dc22
  [B]
                                            2009031092

1   2   3   4   5   15   14   13   12   11   10

Dedicated to John Payne and all the dancers

Linda Grant Niemann

Dedicated to my parents.

A special thanks to my parents for choosing "blue highways" rather than interstates during our "making-time-isn't-important" travels. Roadside distractions, railroaders included, gave personal meaning to "the journey *is* the destination."

Thanks as well to Robert Bannister and Paul D. Schneider for recognizing, supporting, and encouraging a "lawless" approach to photography.

Joel Jensen

CONTENTS

• ACKNOWLEDGMENTS IX

• INTRODUCTION XI

1 BOOMER IN A BOOM TOWN 3

2 BREAKING-IN BLUES 11

3 BLUES FOR RON 17

4 BEET INSPECTOR 25

5 THE BLUE MOTEL 31

6 THE BIG FOUR BAR 35

7 LEARNING SPANISH 41

8 ORGANIZED BOOMING 47

9 THE BORDER 53

10 ON THE ROAD AGAIN 57

• GALLERY 61

11 A STARRY NIGHT 85

12 TRAIN TO THE UNDERWORLD 87

13 BACK TO WORK 93

14 THE HOSPITAL YARD 99

15 THE HOPPER AT GRANITE ROCK 107

16 THE LAWRENCE SWITCHER 111

17 THE LORD OF THE NIGHT 117

18 MIDNIGHT TRAIN TO GEORGIA 127

19 THE SPIRITUAL BEAUTY OF THE RAILS 133

20 OLD HEAD, NEW HIRE 137

• GLOSSARY 149

ACKNOWLEDGMENTS

I would like to thank my readers of this book when a manuscript: Carter Wilson, Donna Hunter, Helen Wallis, Joanne Sterricker, Patricia Henritze, Kay Reeve, and Dorothy Mohr. Thanks to Valerie Dibble for help with selecting the photographs. Also I am grateful to the people who granted me interviews: Pat Doolette, Julie Watson, Bonnie Susbauer, Cary Smith, Howard Halla, Kevin Klein, Ceace Poxon, Joey, Jen Wallis, and Joe Wyman. I would like to thank Al Stockton for permission to tell his story.

I would also like to thank the Burruss Institute at Kennesaw State University for a travel grant and the Center for Excellence in Teaching and Learning at Kennesaw State University for a Faculty Enhancement Leave grant to enable me to have time to finish the manuscript.

The stories in this book are true. In a few cases, I have changed the names of the characters, either at their request or to protect their privacy.

A version of "Boomer in a Boom Town" previously appeared in *Boomer: Railroad Memoirs* (Berkeley: University of California Press, 1990) and in *Trains* magazine (June 2004). © 2009 TRAINS Magazine. Reprinted with permission of Kalmbach Publishing Co. All rights reserved.

Parts of "Breaking in Blues" previously appeared as "Railroad Women Tell It" in *Railroad History* (December 2002), the journal of the Railway & Locomotive Historical Society, and as "Mean Old Nontraditional Blues" in *Railroad Heritage* (March 2007).

A version of "The Hospital Yard" previously appeared in *Trains* magazine (January 2003). © 2009 TRAINS Magazine. Reprinted with permission of Kalmbach Publishing Co. All rights reserved.

A version of "The Lawrence Switcher" previously appeared in *Trains* magazine (March 2005). © 2009 TRAINS Magazine. Reprinted with permission of Kalmbach Publishing Co. All rights reserved.

A version of "The Lord of the Night" previously appeared in *Trains* magazine (September and October 2006). © 2009 TRAINS Magazine. Reprinted with permission of Kalmbach Publishing Co. All rights reserved.

I met Joel Jensen when Mark Hemphill, the editor of *Trains,* put us together, seeing in both our work the same qualities. Before he sent me photographs to look at, Joel sent me a hand-written letter with questions about the story, the main characters, and the mood. The photographs he sent were perfectly in sync with the trajectory of the narrative. It was as if at any moment, one of the characters turned and looked out the window. What he saw was a Joel Jensen photograph.

The literary narratives we collaborated on are included in this book. However, the photographs we selected form their own unique essay. To look at Joel's archive I made a road trip to Ely, Nevada, to meet him in person. After flying to California, I borrowed my friend Carter's old Buick, complete with Van Morrison tapes, and drove from Santa Cruz to Ely. I saw a lot of railroad I used to work on. I even ran into Bob Machmeyer, a fellow conductor on Amtrak, at the Nugget motel in Reno. I told Bob he was in this book, and his comment was, "I hope I have my clothes on." After Reno the road took me up range, down into basin, back up into range. The light was dancing on the dun and grey mountains, a mirage flooding the road ahead.

In Ely, Joel and I spread out photographs on the floor of an old warehouse fronting on the switch yard of the Nevada Northern Railroad. The photographs showed extremes of weather, camaraderie, night work, solitude, bars, decrepit motels, and stark western landscapes. I immediately connected with them emotionally. They all took me back to specific places and states of mind I had been in working as a brakeman in the West. That is why I think of our work as having a shared vision. Joel knows the loneliness of the job and the place.

I called the book *Railroad Noir* to borrow some of the dark, alienated, and hard-boiled elements from the cinematic term. A certain romance attaches to the railroad, but I wanted to signal that these stories give it a twist. Railroad workers often feel a sense of betrayed romance as they confront the realities of their lives. They struggle against inept and arbitrary authority. They work at night in the rain. They cuss. Both the grimy industrial landscape and the starkness of the desert are noir settings to their stories. But the noir elements are not there for style; they are just a part of the complete picture of railroad life, a part that is often omitted in railroad literature.

I experienced railroading as tough on home lives and health. Many people I worked with are gone now, either killed on the job or by collateral damage, due to the lifestyle. As Bob Machmeyer said to me, "You know us, warts and all."

For those readers unfamiliar with railroad lingo, I have included a glossary at the end of the book.

Linda Grant Niemann

Forest ranger, horticulturalist, railroad engineer, or U.S. Marine? An eccentric mix of future career choices, though at 15 years young, one's muses are entitled to all-over-the-map status, professional golfer included. This was the point in life when high school career guidance counselors met with students, studied strengths and weaknesses, and began to template an "appropriate" career path.

A career as railroad engineer or marine furrowed the brows of my counselor and parents. My strength was in the arts—graphic design in particular, something I enjoyed, though unenticing in a 9-to-5 sense. Sitting at a fluorescent-lit, cubicle-enclosed desk held no appeal, nor did staring at a blank piece of paper in need of a creative visual concept. A hand wrapped around the throttle of a 3,000-horsepower locomotive, rather than a rapidiograph, may not have presented the challenge of creating something from nothing, but at 15, testosterone trumped creativity and everything else. Logic or college wasn't in my future equation; railroading was.

It wasn't until the summer of my junior year in high school that naïveté met face-to-face with railroading for what it *is*, rather than what I perceived it to be. Proposed for a family vacation was an Iowa-to-Rocky Mountain National Park detour via Cheyenne, Wyoming. Cheyenne represented Mecca to a kid whose love and fascination for trains was in the blood. Genetically encoded, passed on to and through me by my railroad-loving father, the allure of the railroad couldn't be fought, denied, or ignored. During the Cheyenne campground layover, Dad suggested a post-dinner visit to the nearby Union Pacific depot for an opportunity to "watch the parade of trains and shoot the breeze with crewmen." I could relate to the former, but why the latter?

Within half an hour or so, I was sitting on a baggage cart, preferring to be alone, while Dad struck up conversation with an older head. Drowned out by idling diesels, the discussion between my father and the railroader went unheard, though I suspected "deglorification" of the railroad, my career as engineer included.

It wasn't long before I caught a sidelong glimpse of Dad—now sharing crew change bench space with the railroader—flagging me in their direction. Shit. His name long forgotten, I was introduced to a face forever remembered, handshake and smile not included.

"So . . . your dad tells me you want to be an engineer?"

For whatever reasons, degrees of guilt and embarrassment crept in between my "yes, I do" thoughts and his piercing stare. Eye-to-eye contact caved into an "I'm thinking about it" response and a shoelace that didn't need tying. Youthful awkwardness and a railroader put on the spot came silently between the three of us, though momentarily.

Heart and soul bent on a "don't work for the railroad" lecture, the engineer and my father spoke of higher career ground in a personal regret-and-remorse sense. Neither had gone to college and were nudging me in that direction, further away from the railroad. Whatever lay ahead for me was better than the "hell-on-wheels life of an over-the-road trainman" and what the engineer described as "round-the-clock, never-ending tired, on and off the job," adding, "chances are, if you go to college, you'll land a job that'll find you home at night. . . . And a bad night of TV or whatever will be better than yet another night on the railroad . . . staring down the tracks at a headlight illuminating next to nowhere nothing."

Continuing on, he asked me if a wife was in my future. At 16, marriage wasn't in my thoughts, though a "someday" answer was. He then pointed to several nearby train crews: "Divorced, divorced, divorced twice, shacking up with someone half his age."

He then pointed his finger at his chest. "Divorced after twenty-some years of mostly miserable marriage . . . mostly job related . . . never home, or home enough to make it work. No woman with half a brain would marry an over-the-road railroader. The pay's good . . . the life isn't . . . alone or with another."

Whether or not the Union Pacific engineer influenced my decision to go to college, I can't say for sure. He did, though, succeed at presenting railroading for what it is, in a Linda Niemann manner of speaking. Somewhere along the way, between that summer vacation and enrolling in college, "Cheyenne to Rawlins" and back, over and over and over, year after year, lost its naïve railfan notion of romance.

If there was any one thing that the railroader said, in terms of forever word-for-word remembered, it was a closing comment before boarding his westbound freight. "Between here and Rawlins, the highlight of my four- to twelve-hour shift . . . if I'm four-hour lucky, ha . . . a bunch of antelope trying to beat our train across the tracks. I don't like to see us hit one, but a close call helps to keep us awake. . . . For that matter, so does a kill . . . something to get the blood flowing."

Although college didn't work out in terms of graphic design, a required photography class did, fueling a vision beyond a degree or life on the rails. Since then, the railroad has remained in my blood, recorded from an outsider-looking-in perspective—up close and personal, yet from the "safe distance" of an eye behind a camera's viewfinder. The Cheyenne engineer pre-dated my interest in photography, but he's figuratively here throughout the images in this book, alongside a fellow rail turned author and college professor. Linda's never met him yet knows him in a sense that neither I nor the majority of the readers of *Railroad Noir* ever will.

Somewhere out west, a railroad lonely shared, on and off the train. Somewhere between tears and laughter, longing to be home. Alone or with another, real or imagined, just home.

Joel Jensen

RAILROAD NOIR

ENGINEER. DAGGETT, CALIFORNIA.

"You girls are going to quit the first time it really rains," conductor Wiggins told us railroad women as we were reporting to work one night.

It was 1979, one of the first years that women were hired to work as brakemen/switchmen on the Southern Pacific Railroad. About fifteen years later, I went to his retirement party. It had rained a few times since then, and, that first year, never as hard as it did in Houston, Texas.

I hired out in July in Watsonville Junction, California, but I soon found out railroading was not a year-round job. A conductor I trusted told me to follow the work because I'd never learn the job on the cut-off board. And so, when they laid me off in November, I went booming to Los Angeles, but I soon got cut back to a few yard shifts. There was one place, however, that was going strong, and that was Houston. It was the last year of the oil boom, and Southern Pacific was scrambling to make repairs on its newly acquired Cotton Belt territory and keep the business rolling. When the railroad wants something, there is suddenly a lot of money to be made. In February, Mary Alsip, one of the women who hired out at Watsonville, called me in LA with the boomer news. The railroad was offering free plane tickets, free lodging, free transportation to and from work, and all the shifts you could handle. I looked up Houston in the newspaper. It was 84 degrees. I packed my summer gear and got on the plane. The South was unknown territory to me—so unknown that I even

thought of Texas as the South. Outside the Houston airport I gave the cabbie the name of the boomer hotel and settled into the back seat, feeling like the dangerous stranger who just rode into town.

The Center City Motor Hotel was the establishment the railroad put up trainmen in. Caste distinctions were important here, apparently, for the engineers rated the Holiday Inn. It was one of the quirks of railroading that although the conductor was the boss of the whole train, engineer included, the engineers considered themselves superior because their job was less physical. Trainmen's feet actually touched the ground during a shift, whereas the engineer sat in a chair and related to a machine. In terms of the evolution of civilization, they were on a higher rung. Trainmen, conversely, were fond of pointing to their lanterns and saying to the engineers, "See this light? Well, it's yer brains," referring to the fact that, when switching, the engineer's job was to follow signals and not make any independent decisions to move. It was an old controversy, not likely to be resolved here, although now the two unions are under pressure to merge, kind of like an old cat and an old dog trying to share the same bed. In Houston, however, engineers had considerably better beds than we did, the Center City being located in a downtown whose streets were inhabited by hordes of homeless, also drawn to the city by boom times.

The seedy lobby was full of trainmen with their grips, waiting for rides to work, women in hot pants in the bar, looking as if they were working, and new arrivals like me waiting to check in. I called the crew dispatcher from my room and he marked me up immediately. The phone rang six hours later—on duty for a drag to the port, reporting at Englewood yard. Englewood was an enormous hump yard, meaning that, in addition to receiving and departure tracks, it encompassed about a hundred bowl tracks at the base of a classification hill. A track-full of cars without air was shoved to the crest of the hill and disconnected in various groupings by a switchman walking alongside the cut. The foreman in a tower overlooking the yard gave the switchman the car counts, as well as unsolicited advice. Today, since we were a drag, our only problem with Englewood yard was figuring out how to leave it. With eight months of railroad experience, I was surprised to find myself the foreman. The other switchman, Lloyd, had even less time than I did, although we both had to technically hire out again to work here. He was a boomer from El Paso, and he had arrived at the Center City a few minutes behind me. The engineer was from Oregon. None of us had any idea where the port was or how to get there. The yardmaster, another boomer who had been promoted for getting hit with a puzzle switch, just wanted us out of his hair.

"Just do the best you can," he said, handing me my orders. This was to become a refrain all through my career. An academic in my former life, I believed that you had to know everything before you did anything. In the real world, you just did the best you could.

The other switchmen in the shanty were little help in even locating our train. Luckily, I had spent some time on the main line working in LA, or I would have been even more freaked out than I was. I only had the vaguest idea why trains didn't run into one another. All the hundreds of rules were still alphabet soup in my brain. The general "can do" Texas attitude of Lloyd, the helper, was a good thing.

"Well, we most likely can't go too far wrong if we just go slow," he said.

"Just as long as they don't expect us to actually get anywhere," I said. "I guess we can plod along until we die on the law."

In fact, that was our fate, being unable to work longer than twelve hours under the Federal Hours of Service Act. After creeping forward all day on signal indication in the general direction of the port, we gratefully tied the drag down and waited for the company carryall to bring the relief crew. We were doubly glad to be inside the cab waiting, now, since what Texans call a "Blue Norther" had blown into town.

"Nothin' but sagebrush and barb wire keepin' it back," Lloyd commented. He didn't seem to be any more warmly dressed than I was, but Texans are tough. They rarely covered up even in the rain.

"If you don't like the weather in Texas," Lloyd said, "just wait five minutes. It'll change."

We were all now settled down in a gumbo house knocking back Weller and longnecks. Lloyd was down here with three new hires like himself—Art the bodybuilder, Father Flannagan, so named because he was starting out in his forties, and Rita, a mother of seven. They had hired out in El Paso in the summer and found themselves cut off, as I had, as soon as the winter slow-down hit. Rita was about 5'2" and had a blonde Dolly Parton hairstyle, manicured nails, and wore high heels when she wasn't wearing work boots. Her no-good ex had left her when she was in the hospital with number five, and then she adopted two of her sister's children. Rita was where the money was, and the money was in Houston.

She would come back from an eight-hour yard shift, have six hours before her next call, and spend the time setting her hair in rollers. She worked around the clock, like the men did, but had them convinced she was the helpless type. It was a variation on the "you can't win" theme for women on the railroad. They liked her femininity, but complained about her behind her back. Their wives found her threatening. Surely she was after their men. The wives started making hostile phone calls to her room, telling her to go back home and take care of her children. Of course, bringing home the paycheck was taking care of her children, but doctrinaire types never seem to think the problem through. Rita was a mother; Rita should stay home. Of course, it wasn't OK for a woman not to have children either.

"Say, how come you don't have no kids?" they'd ask me.

"Oh," I'd say, "it's probably because I always read the directions."

That usually won me the poleaxed stare. "You're peculiar, you know that?"

So I decided to hang with the West Texans, the ones who wanted to "put the 'j' back in Texas." We would work as many around-the-clock shifts as we could, and then lay off and party in the country-and-western bars, such as Gilley's in Pasadena. We two-stepped and rode the mechanical bull. We did the "bullshit" dance. We ate mountains of Gulf oysters at happy hour. We ate etouffee, crayfish, and red beans and rice. We bought hats and boots. And we made lots of money. One Monday I was trying to deposit a paycheck between shifts and caught a glimpse of myself in the white-carpeted bank's gold-embossed mirrors. Dirty face, overalls, work boots. The teller was immaculately dressed with 3" heels and 5" hair.

"Say," she said, "do you make this kind of money every month?"

"Every two weeks," I said.

The chemical industry around Houston was working around the clock, as we were, and the railroad was rebuilding track as well as trying to move trains. The tracks both in Englewood yard and in the districts were in bad shape, the rails often resting on rotten ties and swampy sinking soil. Derailments were so common that we never even filled out accident reports unless it happened at speed or someone was injured. The rails would simply spread under your engine and you would feel this familiar bump-bump and the train line would rupture, sending the train into emergency braking. For rookies like us, it was a painless way to learn what could happen, what derailments felt and sounded like, and how to re-rail cars with the engine and blocks of hickory wood. You also stopped being so afraid of making mistakes and let the body start to learn the moves you needed to know in your sleep so that you could function without thinking about everything you did. This was a long process,

first being comfortable around the heavy equipment, which could kill you, and then being comfortable with the way you had to move around it. All your dream time became occupied with figuring this new dance out, often waking you in the middle of a deep sleep sure you hadn't thrown a crucial switch back or certain that the train's brakes were blazing and you hadn't noticed it around the curves. Sometimes when you saw something happen, you would hear an old head's words warning you about that, just the way he had said them, but until that moment the words hadn't locked in for you. I remember hearing the words, "Never turn your back on a cut of cars," seconds after I stepped out of the way of a rolling cut of cars I was trying to couple the engine to. The joint didn't make, and without checking the cut for hand brakes, I turned my back to it and was busy straightening out the engine's coupler when I felt the hair on my neck stand up. I stepped out of the way just as the rolling cars coupled up to the engine. I must have set them rolling when I missed the joint. I never heard them. But I heard the old head's words.

Houston was the first place I used radios instead of hand signals. This meant one person could do all the bowl work of coupling up long tracks of cars while the other members of the crew traded off. Five years later in a contract negotiation, we lost the so-called extra brakeman to these radios. Now though, they were fun and games to the Texas homeboys, a perfect place to air their views on boomers in general and women boomers in particular. One shift I was working the hump, using a radio to direct the engineer to come ahead or back up to couple up some cars we had just humped into one of the bowl tracks. I was struggling to make a joint with a long drawbar on a piggyback auto-rack car. I had my own method of moving them over using my leg muscles instead of my back muscles. As a woman, I had to work out the body mechanics of operating oversized equipment since most of the official ways of doing things didn't work for me. The two couplers had to be lined up so that they met in a handshake when shoved together. It took practice to estimate how to align them when they were the required fifty feet apart. While I was so occupied, the whole yard was providing a running commentary on my progress, actually breaking in on my car counts to the engineer.

"Back 'em up, Sparky, a car length," I said.

"Sounds like one a them California help needs help, haw haw."

"Half a car, Sparky, easy."

"One a them tight underpants help, sounds like, hee hee."

"That'll do, Sparky. Stretch now. That'll do, Sparky. Will you yahoos get off the radio so I can do some work?"

"Oh sounds like you got her riled, hee hee hee."

Shortly afterward, my foreman showed up in the bowl, ready to step in and rescue me. I told him, "Fine, if you want to do both our jobs, I'll go home." He stepped back and stared.

"Well I'll be," he said."You really do care about your work."

I realized I had crossed some sort of personal divide. Raised genteel in Pasadena, California, being impolite was unthinkable. But on the railroad, you had to stand up for yourself, and I credit the Texans for teaching me that. There was no unnecessary job on a railroad crew. You had to trust each other with your life and you had to know whom you could trust. I'd found my sticking point. From then on, it became easier to speak up when I saw a problem or needed to take action fast. Women were trained to hold back, and you couldn't do that here. Pretty soon I was dishing it right back. "You can always tell a Texan," I would say, "but you can't tell them much."

There was an additional ante to the newcomer's game here in Houston—the inherent danger in working with chemical cars. Since the industries were also going full tilt and hiring new help every day, accidents and careless handling of equipment were common. New switchmen in the yard were banging together tank cars with unsecured hatches, releasing chemicals that could land you in the hospital with doctors checking your veins for pockets of trapped gas. There was a sweet odor that hung over the petrochemical switching yards, which, combined with the gas flares being vented into the humid night, gave the place a surreal and ominous character. Employees on bicycles carrying gas masks followed your engine whenever

you went inside a plant to switch. In March, when the work began to slow down in Houston, we new hires were forced to the petrochemical yard at Strang. The homeboys in the shanty were smug.

"Y'all better watch out or they'll be sending you back to California in a pine box."

You couldn't blame them for resenting us. After all, they paid their own rent and transportation. The party at the boomer hotel, however, was now officially over.

My first night reporting to work at Strang was archetypal. Walking into the switchman's shanty when you are extra and don't know anybody is hard for anyone. The regular crewmembers don't talk to you and seem to enjoy your confusion. Being a woman and walking into a new locker room reaches comical proportions. This was true then and it was still true when I left the railroad twenty years later. The only difference is that in today's workplace, the hard-core porn is gone. A few years after the women showed up, the *Hustler* centerfolds came down, but Strang had a variation on the theme that I will never forget.

After being directed down to the bowl tracks by various grunts and nods, a switchman pointed out a series of cabooses on a spur track adjacent to the parking lot. This is where the bowl job I would be working that night reported for duty. Back when jobs had cabooses, a specific caboose might belong to a local, so that the conductor and crew could leave their gear aboard and have a place that felt like home. This, however, was no home sweet home. Every inch of the walls and ceiling was papered with porn. Everywhere I looked was a huge breast or a vulva. The caboose really belonged in a porn museum. No art installation I had ever seen, Keinholtz and Judy Chicago included, even came close. The old boy conductor seemed as eager to get me out of there as I was to leave. What could I say? Men were really weird.

I wondered how the race thing played in the caboose. Men of color had preceded us women in breaking into the operating crafts, and they were still in the minority. A black conductor had told me he was glad to see us women out here, since it took some of the heat off for them. I found another odd piece of porn one night when I went to use the head, located inside the engine compartment. A magazine featuring naked black men was lying around next to the throbbing pistons. The engineer and conductor on the crew got a good giggle out of that one.

Paradoxically, the times I found myself working on an all-black crew, I felt safe and protected. I had the rarest of all experiences, a view from the other side. The railroad did that for me—it took me places and showed me things I never would have been able to see just living my middle-class life. My conductor one night told me that his job before this one had been chopping cotton and that he used to take his lunch to work in a syrup bucket. Now he drove a Cadillac. It reminded me of what one of the women brakemen had told me about her first railroad paycheck. She was a single mother and times had been tight for a long time.

"I took that first paycheck and I went right down to Sears and I bought me a brand new washer-dryer."

I guess I had never really understood what a good job could mean and how hard people would work to keep it.

After about a month, Lloyd and I were allowed to return to the extra board at Englewood yard and we went back gratefully. We moved into an apartment in the Montrose district and were catching a lot of locals and hauler jobs working the small switching yards around the city. As usual, we were completely lost in the new territory. Knowing the maze of tracks is most of the job in railroading. Once you master them, you feel at home, even at 3 AM. Railroad tracks make their own way; they bisect neighborhoods in a totally different way than roads, sidewalks, homes, parks, and the façades of businesses. A railroader knows an entirely different place than the people who live in it. We trespass. We open gates; we go to the loading docks, the junkyards, and the insides of factories and chemical plants. It is an odd feeling of disconnection to cross a street while riding on the end of a freight car. You realize that you are on a different map and that you have no idea of where you are in that neighborhood, in that civilian world. That sense was doubly true in Houston, because I had no access to the normal world there. With no car, I only knew the routes the taxi took to and from work and the streets around the downtown where I stayed. When I had to get out and walk the train to cut a crossing, it was as though I had been set down on Mars. Who were these people in cars, in the houses beside the tracks? Where was I, really?

There were lots of stories to give me pause, about brakemen walking their trains and meeting irate drivers with shotguns, tired of waiting for a crossing to clear. Vandals packed the automatic switch points with rocks, hoping for a derailment. At routine stops kids would surreptitiously turn the angle cocks on the trainline between the cars, making it impossible to move the train. You would then walk back, for a mile sometimes, to cut the air in again, only to have other angle cocks turned behind you. Kids routinely threw rocks at the train, and, in spite of the heat, you learned to keep the windows closed. Sometimes people shot at the train, and sometimes trainmen pulled guns out of their grips and shot back into the night.

At other times, runs would be like vacations in the sun. One day I was called for a hauler to Galveston and saw the Gulf of Mexico for the first time. The hoghead had asked me to run and I sat in his seat, kept the throttle on 3, and opened the window to the offshore breeze sweeping the causeway as we walked on water, rocking toward the island, owning the way. Yarding the train there, we sunk into the sand, the rotting ties hardly held by the spikes, the cars leaning so much we nearly cornered the engine getting around them on an adjacent rail. The place smelled like the sea, but humid and decayed. The oily smell of the Gulf seeped through the sand, coating everything. We deadheaded home in a company van, surrounded suddenly by an aging resort, pastel Victorian cottages sagging in the afternoon, their porch paint faded. Like tired cowboys, we lay back in the van and let the driver drive. A good run and a good day, the pony on the house track, the cars tied down in the yard, that good feeling of being physically tired, with an extra day's pay for the deadhead and the guarantee of a night to sleep in. My brakeman's reward.

May brought with it a heat that closed in on you and torrential rain that would come and go in minutes. Brakemen didn't bother with raingear, since you got as wet in it as out of it. The work was slowing down and one night I got the call at 12:01 AM that I was cut off the extra board.

"You woke me up to tell me that?"

"That's correct," the crew-caller's voice announced.

It didn't break my heart. Beet season was starting in Salinas, and I had survived my first year on the job. I had a carpetbag full of cash, some railroad stories to tell, and skills that had become habits. I jumped when I heard a loud noise or a wave approached me, lying on the sand. I dreamed about tracks and switching moves. I just got up, when the call came in the middle of the night. And I thought of myself as a rail; that was what I was proud of now.

ROLL-BY INSPECTION. MILFORD, UTAH.

Actually, it wasn't so bad breaking into the operating department on the Southern Pacific Railroad. Jimmy Carter was president, the civil rights movement had gathered a decade of steam, and some legal barriers to women's employment had fallen due to lawsuits. Ethnic minorities had preceded us into the crafts of trainmen and engineers, forcing the all-white unions to redefine their ideas of brotherhood. Now they would have to get used to including sisters. Ironically, it wasn't until I had left the railroad in 2000 that a union member called me "brother," but all my union correspondence was always addressed that way. Some women railroaders felt excluded by tokens such as this, but I always felt that until sufficient numbers normalized our presence, the most we could hope for was to be included in the generic. I remember a passenger coming up to me on the San Francisco commutes one day and pointing to my hat, which read "Brakeman." "That should say brakeperson," he said. "Why didn't you tell him that?" I said, pointing to my fellow conductor. Until enough women were doing the job, you did not want to be identified as a brakeperson on the Southern Pacific Railroad.

I guess what I am talking about is prejudice, which I never understood until I started working for the railroad. Prejudices are cherished notions that people do not surrender, even when they are contradicted by the facts. Some of the women who hired out with me would argue politics and feminism with their fellow workers, but I didn't waste my breath. If you were a good worker, they would just think you were the exception. It wouldn't change their ideas. We women were the last hired under the old labor contracts that included a full crew size. Technology, including hand-held radios, end-of-train devices, and centralized traffic control, soon replaced three of the five members of a train crew. The replacement of the engineer by a remote-controlled unit was after my time. The massive attrition in jobs meant that no new trainmen, let alone new women trainmen, were going to be hired for a long time, almost twenty years. This cold fact gradually wore away at the camaraderie we felt during the first years in the late 1970s when we were breaking into the trade. In the San Francisco Bay Area, we would meet and share stories in the spirit of consciousness-raising groups of the 1960s. In my class of seventeen in Watsonville Junction in July 1979, there were three women. In the year before, there were four women. In August 1979 in San Francisco, there were two women. When I was working in 1999 as a switchman in San Jose, I was the only woman operating employee in the whole Bay Area.

Railroad work has always been somewhat seasonal, but you could normally expect to work steadily in your home area after the first few years. This normalcy never occurred for us. The first few years we followed the work, sometimes individually, sometimes as a group of women, from the Bay Area to Los Angeles, Houston, Tucson, Ogden, Dunsmuir, and West Colton. We were boomers because to us the railroad was an unheard-of opportunity to earn good money. Often our male counterparts left the railroad before we did, simply because they could make as good money locally, whereas we couldn't. Women's willingness to move with the work or, later, to be force-assigned to a different location at the whim of the railroad, presented us with the biggest challenge we faced—breaking into a new womanless location constantly and having to deal with the prejudice that went along with that.

Before I go much further, it is only fair to deal directly with this question: Can a woman do the job of brakeman on a freight train? When we hired out, one of the tests all brakemen had to perform was to pick up and carry an 85-pound knuckle for two car lengths. We all did this. In twenty years on the job, I never had occasion to carry a knuckle two car lengths. It would take a real knuckle-head to carry a knuckle that far. What you might occasionally have to do was to change out a knuckle that the engineer had ruptured through bad train handling. In this case, you would walk back to the rupture, disconnect the rear of the train from the cars remaining behind the engine, and tell the engineer to throw a spare knuckle off the engine. You would then climb aboard the cut of cars and instruct the engineer to pull ahead until you were abreast of the knuckle. At that point you would have to pick it up and place it on the drawbar and reverse your movement to the ruptured joint, where you would replace it. The whole operation required lifting the knuckle twice. Any man or woman in reasonable shape could do this, simply by keeping your knees bent and the weight close to your body. It is interesting to note that under the overthrown "women's protective laws," the need to occasionally lift a knuckle would have kept women out of the profession. Women, under these laws, were prohibited from lifting over 50 pounds. Perhaps that is why in every new terminal I went to, some old head would come up to me and ask, "Well, can you change a knuckle?" One idiot even bet me $50 I couldn't do it.

The most difficult physical challenge to women in the work environment was the sizing of the equipment for men. Women had to figure out how to operate the oversized equipment using proper body mechanics. As far as I know, the railroad never did any study on the difference in technique in operating switches and other equipment for men and women. Women were simply instructed in operating equipment the same way men did. I knew this was incorrect from my own training as a lifeguard, in which women were instructed to carry inert bodies around their waists, for example, while men could put them over their shoulders. In approaching railroad equipment, I respected my own center of gravity and used my weight and legs to move drawbars, switches, and brake wheels. I never hurt myself on switches. After all, railroad equipment utilized levers and wheels. All that was required to throw a poorly maintained or damaged switch was increasing the length of the lever. I frequently carried or stashed a piece of pipe that would fit over the handle of a defective switch, enabling me to throw it. The railroad, however, was ultimately responsible for maintaining the switches and equipment so that neither men nor women would unnecessarily hurt themselves operating them.

I suppose the underlying question for women was whether they were willing to take the workplace on the terms they found it, or whether they would invoke special concessions supposedly granted to them socially in the world at large. The men just weren't sure how to treat women on the railroad. A case in point involved the way new trainmen or enginemen learned their trades, namely by making mistakes and listening to the old heads' stories. The formal training period for both crafts was very brief—only two weeks of classroom instruction for brakemen, and all operating crafts started as brakemen. You really learned on the job, and breaking in involved getting other people to teach you. You also learned by making mistakes and getting ridiculed. Perhaps the men did not feel comfortable ridiculing women or perhaps it was a more sinister motive, but when women made mistakes, they were treated as though it was a sign of their unworthiness to do the job.

The old heads' stories gave you information you would never hear in a training class. I was working up in Dunsmuir on the Siskiyou line and we were ascending the steepest grade on the Southern Pacific system. As we entered the tunnel that contained the summit, my old head conductor told me the story of a famous runaway train that reached its point-of-no-return at this very spot.

"You see," he said, his voice like a radio soap in the darkness of the caboose, "the engineer kinked an air hose right after he left Ashland and when he went for his brakes after cresting the summit, he didn't have 'em. The old man [the conductor] knew they were going too fast to get stopped, so he pulled the air and jumped. The brakie wasn't fast enough so he was in for a ride."

"What's kinking an air hose?" I said. They had never mentioned anything like that happening in my class and nobody had mentioned it in the six years I had spent working.

The old head told me that sometimes the flexible hose that contains the braking system on trains gets a kink similar to a garden hose and the braking application can't travel from the engine backward. In that case, the conductor would have to pull the emergency valve in the caboose to send an emergency application forward. As a brakeman, I would have to know to do that in a similar situation. If I hadn't been on that train having that conversation, I wouldn't have known anything about it.

I mention this incident because in 1985 I spoke with a woman engineer out of LA, Jackie McFadden, about an accident in which her brakes failed and she jumped out of her moving train. What she told me illustrates both points—how women are perceived if they are thought to have made a mistake, and how we all learn from experience. Jackie told me:

"Railroad work is dirty, very dirty. You stick your head out that window all the time and you come home with your face and your hair just covered with diesel grime, especially now that they don't take care of anything. When you have to look out the window, you get these cramps in your body because you're in this distorted position. And then you're turning around all the time trying to look for switchmen and also to look for the signals and then the switchmen disappear. That's what pisses me off."

"What do you do then?" I asked her.

"You just slow down and when they start disappearing, you just stop. But a lot of guys have so much confidence in the people they're working with that they don't do that. That's usually when you get in trouble. Then you got people like the one that I punched. He's dingy. He's been in bad motorcycle accidents; I understand he's got a plate; he died a couple of times. Well, I worked with him and he did bizarre things, and this time I got off the engine to tell him that I didn't appreciate him stepping between the cars when I was coming to a joint, because I didn't want to hurt anybody. Every time I got ready to come to the joint he'd disappear. He'd go between the cars. He's going to hook 'em, or he's going to hose 'em up before you even come to the joint. So, I get down off my engine and I'm walking on back there and he's already hooked 'em up and he was up on second unit. I said, 'Look, if you and I get along,' and I didn't finish what I was saying when he called me a nigger bitch. When he said it, you know, it's like he slapped me and it was like a reaction that I just leaned back and I hit him in the stomach. I was right underneath the tower. I stepped down and I was shaking. I got back to the unit and I picked up the radio to call the foreman to tell him about it and as I was doing that he was calling me to say he forgot to tell me about the headman, and I said, 'Well, it's too late.' So, I said, 'You better get up here right now.' He came up and he told me, 'You know, you have to watch him because he's been in a couple of accidents and he's got brain damage and stuff.' Well, he didn't give me no hard time after that. He says, 'Jackie hit me. Tell her to leave me alone.'"

"So tell me about your accident."

"Since the accident I am very, very cautious. So much so that it irritates me. The accident happened to me in 1982 and I didn't get back in service until January 1984. They only cited me for failure to go by the yellow signal at less than 40 miles per hour and failure to stop at the red A signal, but I didn't get back in service until 1984. I am restricted to yard service. The griever wants to ask them if it's OK to let me work locals, so he's even kind of leery about letting me get on the main line, which really pisses me off."

"A woman can't make a mistake."

"No, we can't. As soon as you make a mistake, then it's in the headlines of the *New York Times* and you know that's it from then on. You've had your chance, you blew it. Well, I get to work with two notches on my back, she's a woman and she's a black woman. Plus I've heard, 'Jackie, you have an attitude. You have to be humble,' and I say, 'Fuck it.' You know, who am I to be humble? I can't be humble out here. These motherfuckers will run me over."

"No, you can't be humble."

"Yeah, I'm gonna tell him 'If I don't like you get off my goddamn engine.' You know, 'Don't come in here spittin' that shit on my floor. I gotta walk.' They come in there and they got the little paper cups and they got the slob going down 'em. They need to hang them around their necks like a feed trough. You know, I don't want it in there. That's so disgusting."

"You smoke cigarettes."

"Yeah, you right I smoke cigarettes, but I don't want to step in none of your spit."

"You know, a lot of people wouldn't have gotten back on the engine after the accident."

"I've heard that."

"How did you know to jump? How did you decide?"

"I decided that if it was gonna hit, then I wasn't gonna stay on. I looked out the window and I said, 'I can't jump out this window, no way.' So, I went out the back door and I hung on the steps for the longest time and finally I just stepped off and that's the last thing I remember."

"Now, this all happened in a split second?"

"I guess so; to me it didn't seem like a split second. When I went by the yellow signal, I must have been OK. The speed was coming down 'cause I went by the yellow signal at about 43 mph. I big holed when I went through that second bridge at Montclair, about five units under the second bridge. The brakeman left when I big holed. I thought he'd jumped off, too, because he went out the back door. I didn't know he'd gone out the back door into the second unit. When they didn't find me, they imagined that I was underneath one of the engines. The brakeman immediately ran and shut down the units because they were still running and then he climbed up on my unit and looked in the cab and didn't see me. He saw my jacket and he saw my bag, but he didn't see me. So, he thought that I was underneath one of the units. People came and said, 'There's someone lying back there,' and somebody had come and put seat cushions under my feet. I don't remember any of that. The only thing I remember is waking up and seeing these people leaning over me. He was crying. He was on his knees and he was rocking back and forth. I said, 'Was anybody hurt?' He says, 'No, just you, just you.' I says, 'No, I was going too fast.' He says, 'Shush shush, don't say that; our jobs are on the line.' No wonder he was crying; he was scared to death. I meant I was going too fucking fast to get off.

"They proved that I wasn't going over the speed limit. I knew I wasn't because I had a 55-mile-an-hour train and when I came through Ontario, I was going maybe 54. When I saw the flashing yellow, I immediately started bunching them up 'cause my plan was to bunch them up as I got to the east signal at Montclair. I'd already planned on how I was gonna run this train. I was gonna go through Montclair and Pomona in dynamics, down through Walnut into Industry. That's how my plans were. My plans changed when I got to the flashing yellow, and I remember I said, 'Oh shit.' I throttled down and put about 10 to 12 pounds of jam underneath it and started bunching them up, called the flashing yellow and started bunching them up. And as I went by the flashing yellow, I had bunched them all up and was in run eight dynamics. I went for a little air, went for a little more, went by the flashing yellow, went for a little more, and I had a full service application underneath, and she's still just chook chooka chook chooka, pow, and she's still just going along—'cause usually when you're going into big hole, you can hear the poom. And I didn't hear no poom."

"For the big hole?"

"Right. Then all red. I guess people don't understand that you just can't stop a freight train sometimes, you know? Sometimes you can't even stop light engines. Well, it's hard, it's real hard. I also hear that there are some trains—I've heard other engineers say that they go to give it air and it's just not responding. But if I had been more experienced, I would have known immediately what was happening. Now I can say I know what's happening, because of all I've been through and because of what I listen for now. But at that time I was not experienced and if I'd have been more experienced, I would have

gotten on that radio and told the conductor to plug the train from the rear end."

"Why from the rear end?"

"Because apparently the emergency application didn't go through the train. That train didn't big hole on his end until I hit."

"Could've been a kinked hose."

"I probably did kink a hose when I bunched 'em up—probably kinked a hose, but I don't even know the answer to that."

Jackie found out years later that indeed she had kinked an air hose six cars behind the engine and therefore had only seven cars of operable air brakes. This part of railroad lore she had to learn on her own. She went on to have a long, satisfying career as a main line engineer. When I talked with her in 2004, she was working a plum pool from Colton to Yuma, protected by the New York Dock. In 2008, Jackie died suddenly of lung cancer.

115 DEGREES. DAGGETT, CALIFORNIA.

I rode to work with Ron every Monday, Wednesday, and Friday from Aptos, on the coast near Santa Cruz, eighty miles to Oakland, where we took the California Zephyr from her initiating station to Sparks, Nevada, where we laid over for the westbound Zephyr out of Chicago in the morning. Ron was my conductor and there were two of us brakemen, called by Amtrak "assistant conductors." The terminology bothered me, but compared to "ticket taker" or "utility person," "assistant conductor" was complimentary. Seeing that brakemen's jobs are vanishing, however, I had a bad feeling about seeing the name go, too.

Ron was 59 years old, tall and skinny, with thin auburn hair and a fair, freckled complexion now going mottled in the face due to his being a long-time drunk. He wore round tortoiseshell glasses often hastily repaired, scuffed wingtips with holes, and frayed bow ties. He looked slightly frail, although in true old head style he never missed a day of work. He had hired on in Sparks, Nevada, but moved to California to get away from the influence the gambling atmosphere was having on his kids. Before Amtrak he worked the commutes from San Jose to San Francisco, a job I found deathly boring, but which gave Ron an easy routine to work his drinking into. In the old days, the railroad was a lot more forgiving, and within an easy walk from any shanty was a switchman's bar where you could find most yard crews when they weren't working. That, plus the

ready cash from selling tickets, proved to be Ron's black hole on the commutes.

"Well, you have to be careful not to get behind on your receipts," he'd say. "You have to turn 'em in every week, and it's easy to get behind."

I could see the Ferris wheel in motion on this dilemma—having the ready cash to drink up your receipts and then the mad scramble to make them up from the next week, plus what you drank up then, an endless loop never allowing you to lay off or catch up.

"They got old Wide Load," he said, "for not punching tickets. Caught him dead to rights."

With the railroad crackdown on drinking and the siren temptation of the commutes, Ron had gone over to Amtrak when they took over passenger service from the freight roads. I guess a lot of us were in retreat here. I was hiding out from my local trainmaster's tendency to cut me off the extra board every Monday and call me back to work for the weekend to avoid paying the guarantee that made my extra board job pay my Santa Cruz rent. While I preferred freight, at least passenger work was steady.

On Ron's days to drive he would pick me up in his Datsun pickup and I would throw my grip in the back next to his and climb into a front seat littered with twisted-up pellets of paper napkins— the remainders of Ron's nervous habit of balling up Kleenex into rabbit-dropping-sized pellets and strewing them after him. It was possible to track him on the train by following the trail, like the fabled cookie crumbs in the forest. Ron was usually detoxing in the morning, emitting a ketone-laden alcoholic sweat. I knew the smell because I used to smell like that, too. He would get in a panic over traffic hold-ups or drivers who couldn't take the blood alley Highway 17 curves at 70.

"Why don't these people just stay home? Why do they think they need to go anywhere? Well, I guess we'll make railroad history today. The first time a conductor has failed to show up for his train. The first time in history."

"Plenty of time, Ron," I'd say, watching him carom off the head board in a mock epileptic fit.

In spite of the fact that he worked all the time and obviously spent no money at all on his personal appearance, he was always stashing bill payment envelopes in his glove compartment for mailing at a later time.

"I can mail those on Wednesday when we get back; and I can send that one there off today."

We would cruise by the post office on our way to the Oakland yard and Ron would cut a few off the pile and slide them in the drive-up slot. I couldn't understand where all the money went, but then that is one of those unknowables, as my college advisor told me, along with what your lover is like in bed with someone else. Ron's answer was "major appliances." It was apparently his deal with his wife who, as Ron put it, "didn't get any use out of him anymore." He slept on the couch at home, and she got the credit cards. The Amtrak job kept the system going, let Ron get eight hours of detox every day, pay his Visa interest, and have unmolested drinking time at the turnaround in Sparks.

His credit counselor had tried to get the cards away from him, but the last one he held out on.

"If I could just keep one," he said.

"Pay cash," I told him. "You're paying dope dealer interest. Let go of the cards."

But it was all of a piece. Cash was for drinks; it could disappear mysteriously. Not to be counted on, whereas the Visa card bill was a familiar ball-and-chain.

Ron called his routine "switching the B Street local"—a street of seedy bars in Sparks where he could be found on layovers. His first move in Sparks was to head for the locker he still kept from his brakeman days there and retrieve his quart and a green baseball cap that signaled the transition to recreation. We would all get in the carryall and be deposited at the Nugget casino, where the company put us up. Ron would take the elevator up to his room and ten minutes later he would descend, corked.

"I go to my room and I drink eight ounces of vodka," Ron would say.

The amateur drinkers on the crew would run him off from their spot in the Nugget sports bar, since Ron was a weepy drunk. I ran into him outside the casino after one such altercation. Main Street Sparks was an unreal location enough, a kind of Disneyland Main Street with old-style street lamps, impossibly clean sidewalks, and antiquey saloon signs, now in November lightly dusted with snow. Ron grabbed my arm as if I were a long-lost chum, not at all the ordinary person he rode to work with each and every week.

"They said I overstepped my bounds, telling Lowwater not to speed in Tunnel Five. By God, I know this run; I've been working it for thirty years, and he was over speed. Fine mess we'd have derailing and blocking freight from Klamath Falls to Salt Lake City."

"Oh well, Ron," I said, "Amtrak's got the hogheads thinking they're the boss now. Pretty soon they won't have conductors at all—just let the chief do everything."

"That's right, we're morphedites out here," he said, tearing up.

I think he meant we were not quite trainmen and not quite onboard employees. But his language startled me. I wondered if he knew I was bisexual and was telling me something about himself. But I just nodded yes. He might have been referring to our lot in life also, living like transients yet clinging to the articles of the stationary—houses that other people lived in, cars that other people drove, children that other people took care of.

"But you," he said, clutching my arm, "you're kind. I know I can count on you."

"Sure, Ron," I said, knowing what he meant—that I was an alcoholic, too, but in the program. He knew I'd been in his shoes.

His life had a mechanical life of its own. After switching the B Street local until 3, he would return to his room. Unfortunates next door would hear him diving into an empty bathtub or throwing up wretchedly until dawn. At 7, in uniform and shredding napkins, he would collect himself for the return trip. We would follow the pellets on the carpet to the Nugget carryall that took us to the train.

"Well, right over left, it's one day closer to the box," he'd say, sitting down in the diner to count tickets.

His language was a wonderful mix of southern preacher, self-taught historian, and malapropism. Ron's plans for retirement included buying a motor home and visiting historical sites across America. I doubted he'd last long enough to use it once. Working was the only thing keeping him alive. But he had clearly done a lot of reading, which set him apart from most of his fellow rails. I felt sympathy for him trapped by both drinking and a working-class life. During the days I would drive us, on the way home from Oakland Ron would start to disintegrate, having to endure the rush-hour commute traffic until he could get to the Liquor Barn at home. He would bang his head against the roof of the truck in time with the music or simply start to sing marching tunes. It was like seeing the insides of a clock explode. And then I would drop him off at his suburban home and drive down the road to mine, all the time wondering what the hell we were both doing this for, anyway.

Not drinking hadn't solved all my problems, by the way, as I was sure it wouldn't solve all Ron's. For one thing, I seemed to need a Visa card ball-and-chain too, although I kept it paid off. But it ate up all my cash and kept me tied to the job, so that any dreams of writing full-time had to be kept on hold. It gave me an eerie feeling to see Ron hold the mirror up to my life and it made me realize how on the surface my solutions were. He was like my portrait of Dorian Gray, my diseased persona working beside me every day, other than me, and yet below the surface I was sure the same. When you get sober in the program, they tell you the cautionary story of the progression of the disease, kind of like the cautionary stories told to new hires on the railroad about getting coupled up in the freight yard and calling loved ones to hear your final words before they separate the cars and kill you. The program version is that the disease progresses like a second self even after you stop; and if you start again, you will suddenly be where you would have been if you kept on. You would wake up inside your portrait of Dorian Gray. And here I was working with my diseased persona every day as his helper on the train.

I had already done penance, as I saw it, by working the Reno Fun Train off the extra board all the previous winter. It was a special charter leaving Oakland at 5 PM and arriving in Reno at midnight. The passengers then spent two nights gambling and boarded the train again in the morning of the third day for a return trip. My first trip we had a woman fall down on the platform in Reno, after drinking all day on the train, in an epileptic fit. The paramedics came and hauled her away and I was surprised to see her board the train for the return trip, which she also spent drinking. The scene was replayed at the platform in Oakland, same fit, hauled off again by different paramedics. The problem was that we had no control over the amount of booze on the train. Passengers would board in Oakland with rolling coolers full of hard liquor. The Fun Train, like every other train traversing Donner Pass, had a top speed of 25 mph, so that by 10 PM the passengers were roaring drunk, hanging out of the vestibules, sticking their heads out the windows. I would admonish them sternly, making pantomimes of decapitation, but to no avail. I was a party pooper. I was mean old Heidi in a conductor's suit. Generally, the other conductors didn't mind the action as much. For one thing, they usually had half the train coming on to them, while all I got was the woman-in-uniform macho challenges. I usually gave up on it all and locked myself in the attendant's room, far from the madding crowd. By Reno, most of the train was comatose and relatively quiet. Nobody killed themselves; I guess it was a successful run. I would show up at AA meetings in Santa Cruz with my tales of the Fun Train, and people would stare at me as if I were from Mars. For one thing, having a job in Santa Cruz made you a social outcast. The idea that you would put up with something like this because it was your work was a completely foreign idea.

"You don't understand," I'd say. "I'm the baby on the extra board. Besides, God wants me on this Fun Train."

That usually did the trick. I was there for a reason. I thought of it as my instant karma in play once again. I had played for years in other people's workplaces. Now I would see the other view. Eventually though, my fellow rails took pity on me and let me work the baggage car in peace.

"Say, Linda, why don't you not suit up and just work bags?" Glen, my ladies man conductor would tell me. Drunken women were no problem for him.

"Hallelujah," I said, and bags became my permanent spot. Now, however, on the Reno train regularly with Ron, another deeper aspect of my former life was surfacing.

I had spent the last two years writing the story of my life, and I knew that I would get it published. In it I had gotten honest about a lot of things, drinking, drugs, and my love affairs with both men and women. I had been in and out of the closet for twenty years, but on the railroad it had just seemed too risky to add another layer of difference to being the only woman on the job. The price had been

that I rarely got close to the people I worked with, but, with sobriety, my defenses were cracking. The writing had taken me in advance of where I actually was, and I was feeling pressure to live up to it. Every time I let a homophobic remark by one of my fellow conductors go unchallenged or changed pronouns when talking about what I did last weekend, I felt ashamed of myself.

I even brought my lover with me on the train, as all my fellow conductors did, but I let it look innocent, even though we locked ourselves in the handicapped sleeper downstairs and strung up Christmas lights for the summit ride down to Reno in the snow. Betty charmed them all at dinner with her stories of war reporting in Nicaragua, and in my room at the Nugget we awoke at 3 AM to hear the sad plodding footsteps of the casino's trained elephant, Bertha, as her handler walked her around the concrete parking lot. Bertha dragging her chains. The fact that Betty wanted it this way, too, told me it would never last. But it was the easier, softer way, and I still chose it.

"Morphedites are shunned by all societies," Ron would say, "as they should be, of course, because they go against the upright way."

But there would be a tone of sympathy in his voice, and I wondered what identification he felt. In that odd way secrets have of willing out, one morning as we were sitting down to count the tickets as the Zephyr pulled up Donner grade, I opened an Amtrak ticket envelope and found myself staring at a detailed photograph of my vagina. Luckily Ron was nodding off into his soup at the time or he would have had a coronary. I had taken that picture, years before, when I discovered photography during a particularly hot love affair. It was my Judy Chicago moment with my vagina, immortalized and printed in my home darkroom in the redwoods. Of course, drying prints is a problem because they curl up, and so the portrait of my pussy found its way into *Webster's International Dictionary* to be pressed. Years went by and a few of those prints remained sequestered, until one day when my new kitten, Boomer, attacked the open dictionary and destroyed all the Ws. As I was rescuing it, the picture of my pussy fell out and I slipped it into whatever envelope was close at hand. It turned out the envelope was an Amtrak ticket envelope, which months later found its way into my briefcase and onto our train.

"Egad," I said, waking up Ron and turning cinnabar.

My vacation was coming up in March and I was gone for a month, kayaking the San Juan River and meeting Betty in the desert afterward for some more secret love. She had broken up with me the month before when it occurred to her we were getting serious. Of course, she then changed her mind. Once again, I had been outmaneuvered and was basically responding to whatever direction she gave. The good thing was that all those months working bags had enabled me to paddle the river effortlessly day after day, the sun washing the canyon colors grey, and the morning moisture releasing the acrid sage smells that blended so well with sweat and the outdoors and being happy in your skin. Passenger service seemed far away; I had exploded out of that thin shell filled with hungry fretting people. I didn't think of Ron the whole time I was away.

My first run back, Ray, the rear brakeman, took me aside.

"I'm really glad you're back. Ron had a hard time without you. He got confused and took the pouch off the train with him. They had to carryall it to Salt Lake. I've just about had it with him, messing up. I told him if I catch him drinking on the job, I'll turn him in."

Ron seemed more frazzled than usual. He complained about the extra brakemen he had while I was gone. Claimed it upset his routine. Being a valued crewmember was new for me since I had never been able to hold a regular job before. I was always the extra brakeman.

"And that Ray, he should treat me with more respect. I should say something to him about that. He was quite vehement in talking to me."

All I could do for Ron at this point was to tell him about my trouble sobering up, just fill in the details that were sure to ring some bells with him, terminally unique as he claimed to be. I just kept talking about my struggles and let him see me show up sober every day.

"I just don't think I could sit in those meetings," he would say. "They seem so organized. They might work for some people, but what would I say? I don't even know those people."

"I don't know, Ron," I would say. "I can only tell you what worked for me."

Soon after, I got bumped off Ron's crew and I bid in the Reno/Klamath Falls relief job, making two runs to Reno every week and a brutal twelve-hour all-night haul from Oakland to Klamath Falls. The good part was that I got to watch both Donner Pass and Mount Shasta out the baggage car window, particularly on moonlit nights when Shasta's high serene cone shadowed the train a hundred miles from Shasta City to Klamath Falls. I had grown up hiking the Sierra Nevada, and the high, cold meadows always felt like my first discovered home. I had found a publisher for my book and I was struggling over permissions with one of my characters. I had sent him a chapter and received a threatening letter from the biggest law firm in San Jose. Since he was basically broke, it was a safe bet that he was paying them in wine from his winery. Since I was basically broke also, I had found a rail buff lawyer and I was paying him in rides on Amtrak. I clued the crew in on the deal and they went out of their way to make him and his wife feel like VIPs.

"Oh hi, are you going to defend Linda's book? Well, come on back to the crew room and meet everyone."

Brad and Nina boarded the train like everybody else, but as soon as we got underway, Glen found an unoccupied first-class cabin for them and when we reached Colfax, just before the climb to Donner Summit, I escorted Brad up to the engine and watched him climb the ladder into the cab. Nina later told me it had been the thrill of his life. Of course, we invited them to eat with us in Sparks and my fellow rails couldn't help showing off a little.

"You people don't really carry guns around like Linda says, do you?" Nina asked.

There was a universal reach for their grips.

"Ya wanna see 'em?"

"No, no," Brad said quickly. "I don't want to know."

What with the general boasting, and perhaps the imminence of disclosure anyway via my book, I told the crew a story I had never shared with anyone on the railroad. It was about visiting my lover Clark, whom they'd met, in New York and being late for the plane. This meant I had to carry on the bag I had planned to check—the bag full of all the sex toys I had acquired while volunteering for the San Francisco Sex Hotline. Clark was a bisexual man and he was going to be the recipient of a huge latex dildo, a pump action can of lube, a Hitachi magic wand with attachments, various leather items, stockings, g-strings, feather dusters—the whole nine yards. Apparently my bag looked odd to the X-ray machine and I found myself facing a young, blonde, uniformed inspector on her first day of work. She unzipped my bag, looked in, blushed, and froze. The first thing she fished out was the can of Astro Glide. She turned to ask her supervisor, a black man, what to do and then thought the better of it. Luckily, I had a hotline card and I flashed it and said: "I am a sex expert. These are my demos." And she waved me through.

There was a surprised silence in the Nugget dining room. Who had a better story than this one? Exchanging glances with the engineer, Ray the rear brakeman said, "Well, do you know what happened when Ron took the pouch off the train? He left his grip on board, too. They had to open it and when they did they found, well, items like yours."

"An iron bra," the engineer volunteered, "and pictures of Ron in it."

Railroad gossip being what it was ("Telephone, telegraph, tell a rail," we said), it was nothing short of a miracle that nobody had told me this story before. It showed how shocking they thought it was—something a woman couldn't be told about. And yet, looking around the table, I realized that they accepted this about each other. They all had their secrets, too. Nobody wanted to have some company official or airport security go through their grip. As a matter of fact, when Clark took me to the airport on my return trip, the metal detector picked up the spoon he had lifted from the cafeteria. And I thought about Ron in his room at the Nugget, getting at least some kind of love, becoming a morphedite indeed. Maybe he at least could find some pleasure in that room before crash landing in an empty tub.

I hoped so. My room in Sparks was sterile enough. Apart from the one time Betty accompanied me, it was sex for one.

Ron came to my book party in April, even though it was Saturday and he would have to lay off. That meant missing a round trip, or a third of his weekly pay. I appreciated the compliment for what it was. Wearing a short-sleeved plaid shirt and chino pants, he was the only rail there and, even with his blown capillaries, he looked tougher somehow than my academic friends.

"It's just amazing," Ron said, "the way you have of saying things. You really got those officers, all right. You really got them. Officer Mohan had a red nose. Boy, I'd like to be there when Mike Mohan reads that."

I had naïvely substituted the name Mohan for a dipsomaniac trainmaster in my book, not realizing that Mohan was a former big cheese of the Southern Pacific. I just let Ron think I knew. I felt a wave of affection for him, seeing him venture afield from his well-trodden paths. He looked both peeled like a grape and at the same time wildly free, looking about as if he were a condor contemplating flight.

The next time I saw Ron was in a residential detox program. His crew had turned him in and he was newly sober. He left a message on my answering machine asking me to a meeting and I joined him in the circle I had come to feel at home in. We got the chance to speak in turn and I told him I loved him and I was glad to see him there.

His turn came and he called me a "fine lady." These turned out to be our last words.

I was in Mexico when he died a year later. I missed the funeral but I called Bob Machmeyer, who had taken my place as Ron's brakie. Bob was one of the Viet Nam vets who had been lucky enough to emerge from that horror with an increased capacity for compassion. He told me Ron had gotten his divorce but relapsed into drinking after he retired. He went to a doctor who didn't ask about his alcohol intake and prescribed barbiturates. Ron overdosed.

"That thing with his suitcase," I said. "Did it really bother him?"

"He didn't want you knowing, that was all," Bob said. "He used to talk to me at times about the pleasures of constriction, even showed me a catalog. I'd just say 'Fine Ron, whatever you say.' We went up to the coffin to try to put his hands right, you know how he'd say 'Right over left, one day closer to the box,' but we were too late. By that time rigor mortis had set in."

Bob paused. "Poor Ron," he said. "All alone with a corset and a jug."

"Blues for Ron," I said.

The following spring, I was working freight again on a little switching local that worked the old Milpitas branch out of San Jose. Mostly unused, it had turned into wino alley, crossing the Guadalupe River, where all those breakfasting at the City Lights Ministries came to bathe and wash their clothes. In Silicon Valley, one of the most expensive areas in the United States, the railroad right-of-way is home to many day laborers. They form their camping groups, pulling old mattresses to within inches of the main line, using the conveniently constructed iron railroad bridges as toilet stalls and mini condo units. The Guadalupe River always seemed to me a pastoral sight before we reached the warehouse and junkyard district. It was, in its way, as beautiful as the beach at Rio Del Mar, where the

Silicon Valley dot-com hopefuls were now pitching their million-dollar tents. A fire had charred the bridge foundations, and I always wondered how thorough the railroad's testing procedure had been.

"After the fire," an old head had told me, "them officer bastards sent us across with our train and I saw them hiding in the bushes watching to see if the bridge would hold or not."

The speed limit in the district was 25 mph, but we had Roadie as our engineer, a young cowboy boot–wearing hotshot who had just fathered his first son. Roadie would give you all you asked for, in terms of speed. Consequently, we were rocking down the rails in the Five Zone, rocking through the old and ultra-modern pueblo of San Jose downtown when I saw a small pink globe floating above the shopping cart–strewn right-of-way before us on the main line.

"Ease 'em down, Roadie, there's something on the rails."

As we got closer the pink balloon remained suspended four feet above the right rail, attached to the wrist of a sleeping form huddled up to the main line as if it were a feather pillow. Laying on the horn, as we now were, the figure barely stirred, now appearing to be a young woman with corn-colored hair, cradling a quart of Colt 45 like a baby in her arms. As we got to within a few feet of her, Roadie reluctantly hit the air brakes and the horn simultaneously. Grudgingly, without opening her eyes, the woman rolled away from the train, the pink balloon following her like a power line marker as she came to rest in the weeds beside a chain link fence strewn with litter.

"Goddamn," the crew said in chorus. She was a regular. Some rails had even begun fantasizing about rescuing her from the life. As we passed her, I wondered about the pink balloon. Had some saving soul tied it to her arm? Was it a loving touch, a joke, or had that shepherd part of her tied it to her own arm, knowing what the future was likely to be?

CONDUCTOR IN BLIZZARD.

KNIFE RIVER, NORTH DAKOTA.

In Salinas Valley, beet season is in the spring. Trucks move the turnip-shaped sugar beets to trackside loading centers, where they ride conveyor belts up to funneled loading chutes, filling up old rusty gondola cars that are never used except during beet season. These ancient cars have rotting wooden slats along the sides of the cars, and the beets inside soon start to ferment, filling the already humid valley night with a sour intoxication. They tried to improve the cars once, by making them out of metal, but the beets rotted so quickly that they couldn't be transported. So the old cars remained in service. Their hand brakes were the old kind, called staff brakes, and the torque on them could literally throw a brakeman off the car. You had to wind the brake wheel up with your hand outside the wheel, always hanging on to a ladder rung with your other hand (hence the saying, one hand for you, one for the company), and when it was wound tight, you used your foot to apply the metal stop, called a dog, that kept the wheel in its groove.

My friend Mary Alsip was untying one of these brakes one time and the torque pulled her into the brake and knocked out her two front teeth. Of course, she kept on railroading. Mary kept railroading after a broken neck in a car accident and until she was nine months pregnant. We joked her kid would be the first person to be born with a switch key in his mouth.

It was the spring of 1987. I had just come back from a stint working first Amtrak and then the commute trains that ran from San Jose to San Francisco on the peninsula. Now I was back home in Santa Cruz, working out of Watsonville, where I had hired on in 1979. To the home guard I would always be the clueless blonde who couldn't figure out which way a track was lined, in spite of the fact that as a no-seniority boomer I had seen more of the railroad than anyone working there. First impressions.

The beet hauler went on duty at 8 at night in Watsonville. Its job was to pick up all the loaded beet cars that other jobs had left on sidings in the districts and haul them down the valley to Santa Margarita, the last siding before the grade over the summit at Cuesta, a run of about 150 miles, not counting the return trip with the engine. At Santa Margarita, a job from San Luis Obispo would pick the cars up and continue the shuttle down the coast. The hauler was an easy job with a lot of miles and it drew a high-seniority crew: the oldest hoghead, McCarthy, conductor Johnny Jensen, and brakemen Jessie Flores and Jim Bassman.

There was a problem with the run, however. Since the cars were in such dilapidated condition, the dispatcher had slapped a 35 mph speed restriction on the train and required that a "beet inspector" position be put on to follow the crew in a truck and roll the train by, making a visual inspection of the brakes at certain specified locations, checking on the speed and making sure the old brakes weren't heating up and sparking. Kind of an extra appendix position. A typical railroad situation. Cars too dangerous to use, but use them anyway and if anything goes wrong, it's your fault. Of course, the crew wasn't going to run 35 mph from Watsonville to Santa Margarita because if they did, it would take them twelve hours and they wanted to be going home light engine way before that. So that put them in an adversarial position with whoever was so unlucky as to be called off the extra board to be the said beet inspector.

There was so much wrong with this deal that I couldn't quite fathom it when the fat trainmaster handed me the keys to a beat-up Datsun and said, "Follow that train." The crew, meanwhile, united and transformed from a congregation of four perfectly decent people into a juvenile gang, had already heaped more absurd tasks upon me.

"Hey," Jesse Flores said, thoughtfully, "she can get our siding switches for us."

"Great idea," Bassman added. "And we could have coffee at Santa Margarita. There's an IHOP open all night. You could stop there and get it for us."

McCarthy, a hoghead of the women-belong-in-the-kitchen persuasion, merely snarled my way, before adjusting his baseball cap. No girl beet inspector was going to tell him how to run his train.

Jensen, a rather courtly cowboy, merely looked bemused.

Now there are several things wrong with the idea that a truck can follow a train. First of all, trains run on tracks and trucks run on roads and the two are not always parallel. Secondly, I did not grow up in Salinas Valley, unlike every other member of the crew, and I did not know which little crossroads led to which siding in the middle of an artichoke field, as they did. I knew where the sidings were if I was on the main line, but how to get to them from a highway in the districts, no way. And it was night and it was going to be a long night.

Salinas, California, is not the coolest place to be poking around at night if you are a woman. Mike Serat, an engineer, once told me he had interrupted someone on the tracks in Salinas rolling a drunk for his boots. The guy had checked out Mike's size and grudgingly backed off. Around Alisal Street, across from the depot, was a junkie alkie underworld, with weird denizens appearing out of the fog,

staggering across the tracks and taking up residence in about any cavernous structure not boarded up. This sweet location was my first helper task, to unlock a gate and a switch so the crew could come in and pick up some beet cars. At least I knew where it was, and by then I had figured out how to drive the truck. Jensen met me at the switch after I had the crew lined in and looked around at the reeling drunks across the street and looked at me. I could tell he had warring instincts. Leaving a lady alone in such circumstances was not the cowboy way.

"This ain't the place for a woman alone at night," he muttered.

It would have been safe for me if I had been on a crew, though, because the railroad space belonged to its workers. That was what we believed and acted as if it were true. I would have been bonded with three other people and if I disappeared, they would know immediately. Not that some weirdo couldn't knife you, as happened to Tony Buksa. But he had confronted someone and broken an unwritten rule of silent détente. If you were recognized as a railroader, the bums avoided you, conceded the space to you, because you were the railroad and they the trespassers.

But the beet inspector was just a woman in a truck, where she wasn't supposed to be.

"Yeah," I said. "Have to agree with you this time."

Off to the next roll-by site. Now I had to confront some obstacles placed there by my own personality, my Girl Scout Pasadena persona who was earnest about things, and in this dumbass way, stubbornly persistent. I was told to roll them by. I was going to do it. Of course, I could barely keep up with highballing McCarthy and I was going 50. That asshole no way was doing 35. Did I have to try to slow him down? What about the beet cars? Were they really that dangerous? I tried to think about what my friend Larry Gamino would have done. Larry just did not get stressed. He probably would have driven the beet truck directly to Burger King and had dinner, turning off his radio. Then he would have appeared at the roll-by site, magically in touch again. Then back to Burger King, incommunicado. Maybe he would have gotten them coffee, but probably after two roll-bys, he would have headed for home. "Sorry," he would have said, "I just couldn't find you guys." That would have placed him inside the joke, another trickster, not the victim.

I couldn't get out of the loop. It did bother me to be driving around the valley by myself at midnight. I had taken the McCarthy challenge personally. I was hooked.

The absurd situation had dropped me into a familiar one, being a new conductor in the caboose with a speeding engineer at the head of the train. If he got caught, I got fired. But I can't get on the radio and say "slow down," or we get fired. I can say "riding kind of rough back here," the code for "slow down." But if he is needling me, then he won't slow down. Then my only next move is to pull the air, putting the train into emergency braking, and that is an event I have to report to the dispatcher. I never wanted to take an authority tussle to that level, but I believed all of the old heads would have. In a minute. This was a blank space inside myself I was looking at and it bothered me. On the railroad, the code was that disputes were handled without involving management. You couldn't let an argument become visible, or have visible effects, or you would be considered a rat fink. For a woman, this was especially important. But how did you negotiate stuff like this? I had no clue.

The next pickup was at a siding near King City and again, I was having trouble finding it at night from the road. McCarthy was complaining like a grandmother at the delay and Jensen had finally had enough.

"This is bullshit," he said, getting in the truck with me. "I know where these switches are; let's go."

"Highball," I said.

Both the highway and the tracks followed the Salinas River now as it dove underground, marking its path with cottonwoods and alders and a wide, sandy riverbed. The train entered the tunnels and passed the oil derricks at Wunpost, lit up electrically in the foggy darkness. Jensen's presence calmed me down, and by the time we got coffee for the crew and met up with them at Santa Margarita, I was in another state of mind. Jensen climbed back on the engine, handing the coffee to Bassman and Flores, who now resembled puppies more than tormentors.

"Take it easy on the way home," Jensen said.

"Thanks for the coffee," the puppies yapped.

"Come on, come on," McCarthy griped, ever in character.

The engine set off into the fog, and the boys were gone. Now I could head for home. It was 5 and still dark and the cold fatigue set in. I knew I had failed in some way and been rescued, but I still had a highway to drive and my day wasn't done. The Datsun was a yard pickup and rattled as if its thin shell were going to unbolt itself. I actually hated driving, my usual phobia to being on the grid with everyone else, and now at daybreak morning traffic was beginning to accumulate past King City. The suburbs of San Jose were being pushed farther and farther south, as people sought houses they could afford. Farmland was turning into blocks of condos, side by side with agribusiness. The sixteen-wheelers shared the road with morning commuters in subcompacts. I hated being in this truck. I belonged on the rails that now were two parallel glints in the rising sun.

What I was feeling was exile, banishment from the safety of the train, an odd concept, considering how dangerous it was. But was it? Railroad space was like the space of a village set against a jungle. In the village, space has an order, a ritual, a hierarchy. Hence my struggles with McCarthy the night before. The light engine setting off for home looked like a clipper ship on rails, self-contained and protected. On an engine or on a train, you were able to move around, to be natural in your body, as you would on board a ship. Not strapped into a tin can hurtling forward and able to be thrown in any direction at any time by chance.

The sun now rising like a nuclear oven in the east flashed light stripes in a strobe effect across the road, through the windbreak eucalyptus to either side. I had a dry taste in my mouth from the adrenaline of the night before and my eyes were sandbags I had to continually try to keep blinking. This stretch of Highway 101 was a gauntlet of light and bug-like cars until I felt the softness of grass under the wheels and I corrected just in time to pull the tires back from their desire to flip themselves and me and return to junk from whence they came.

I pulled the truck over and sat there awake for a minute or two. The danger sensors from the night before aligned themselves in my mind. Then I curled in a ball in the front seat and slept until the heat building in the cab woke me hours later and the landscape had the normal feel of a Salinas Valley day. I tied my job up on twelve hours and headed for home, planning to sleep through the call if it came again that night. My dangerous game had been to get too tired without the invisible net that held me safe, somewhere in the fabric of my railroad life. I wanted to memorize this fault line in case I ever felt it opening again, so my body would know it, even if I did not, and warn me.

ENGINE HOUSE. EAST ELY, NEVADA.

Winter layoff, slow time on the board, I drove to Bakersfield then out to Ridgecrest, to a Bureau of Land Management mustang roundup, my new distraction from trouble in mind. In the cold white afternoon, I got restless and had to drive somewhere, outrun the blues I felt coming on. I drove and drove down Panamint Valley, tan and chocolate and white, long string of Southern Pacific grey hoppers at Trona, a Kerr-Megee chemical plant, white salt heaps on the dry lake bed, listening to Patsy Cline, Tracy Nelson, filling up with the blues. I knew I wouldn't feel at home when I got home either, as soon as I caught up with myself. So I turned up the mountain road to Lake Isabella. With the sunset, I calmed down, the terra cotta hillside dusted with snow, dark green of the Joshua trees, white-capped sierra teeth behind them.

I decided to give tomorrow a chance by staying the night at Isabella, chose a cheap room, a blue room with red bedstead, brought in my El Paso blanket, Tarahumara woven wool, with grey and black heavy stripes, so I could turn off the dusty heat in the room. The sizzler restaurant scared me, the sulfite salad bar, so I ate in the Mexican one, a smoky room with small town nosiness, their January despair thick in the air. I ate a poisonous stew, came back to my room to be sick while the wind blew outside.

Morning came, though, the blue room warmed slightly, after a safe night with no dreams. Reading Tennessee Williams's *Field of Blue Children*, I felt better somehow, as if I were home on the rails.

Booming throughout the Southwest, I now felt uncomfortable not moving. When I was home, I was always ready to jump in my truck and drive, particularly when I felt an emotion coming on. Well, it was growing up in LA, too. We went to the freeways to think things through. Just drive. I was used to funky railroad motels. In some places, the company built their own modules, but mostly they had a deal with a local place, like the Resetar Hotel in Watsonville, where I hired out. Rails need a separate wing so we can sleep during the day and stain the carpet with diesel from our boots. The crew callers had to be able to reach us at any time, and if there were no phones, a shagger came over from the depot and banged on the door to give us our call.

I stayed in these places when I was away from home on a turn. After our crew got off a through freight, we waited in turn for another freight, going the other way, to work home. Sometimes the crews would pile up at the motel and eventually, the company would have to deadhead most of us back to our home terminal.

Company motels in the desert were lonely places, and the only company to be found was in the bars that usually sat next to them. Most restaurants were really bars. A lot of western towns had three establishments: a gas station, a motel, and a restaurant-bar. Outside, the treeless glare and 100-degree heat made any sane person look for shelter.

Many rails who wanted to follow the work owned campers or travel trailers, and they would park them in the freight office lot and use the showers at the crew shanties to clean up. The bums under the bridge would be washing up at the water faucet, and the brakemen would be stumbling out of their campers to wash up inside.

Julie Watson, a Southern Pacific conductor, remembers booming.

"I was the only woman in the parking lot in LA. You see, lot of the younger railroaders are boomers, people who travel around to work wherever the work is, and a few railroad terminals allow people to take their trailers, campers, or vans and stay right there in the parking lot so they don't have to spend money on rent. Usually it's temporary, though I have known people to have been there for more than a year or even people from that same area who have moved out because they split up with their wife and didn't want to pay rent. I was in the situation where I didn't have a good place to stay, so I stayed in the parking lot in my camper. The guys who live there are always walking around in their thongs and shorts just talking to everybody. It's the parking lot mentality—no lawns to mow, no chores to do, no rent to pay. The guys I hung around with were from San Luis and they were somewhat protective. They would warn me about lustful guys to watch out for. I remember talking to someone I had just met and this guy came by and said, 'Now you remember she's got eleven older brothers.' He meant my friends from San Luis.

"To take showers I discovered a woman's locker room a mile's drive from the parking lot. I guess that would sound strange to most people. You go down and live in the back of your truck and you take showers that you drive a mile for. To go to the bathroom in the middle of the night, I had to get up and put on my pants and trudge across the parking lot. Usually I have this nightgown on and I had to stuff it down my pants and put my jacket over it.

"When they wanted me to come to work, they do what's called shagging; they come knock on the door. Everybody had their names on their trailers so they knew where to find you. Eventually they got too lazy to come shag people like they were supposed to and they would just beep us on our beepers.

"I never figured out the exact expense of being there but I know we sure didn't have much to show for it. All our expenses were write-offs—mortgage write-off, away-from-home expense write-off—but we were spending money. It wasn't all on paper. I was just not willing to put out $1,200 to move into an apartment. I would need to pay first and last and put out a deposit and in LA they don't like giving it back. A lot of people down there require a nonrefundable cleaning deposit and they assume that when you move out they will take that money whether you were clean or not. I figure LA is the last spot I can usually work with my seniority. I haven't tried El Paso or anywhere else out there to know if there is some place that's more of a last place than LA, but I don't think so."

ROUNDHOUSE WORKER. GLENDIVE, MONTANA.

The one time I found a lover who understood my work was when I met Veronica, the San Francisco police sergeant. Never mind she was drop-dead Italian gorgeous in that cop suit. She knew what work is. No whining about schedules or lack thereof, no drama-filled moments just before I caught my train. It helped, though, that I had a regular run. I deadheaded up from Santa Cruz to work the midnight train back from the city Friday, then the morning train Saturday arriving at noon and the midnight train back, which left us twelve wonderful hours in the city to play. Sundays I worked a double on duty at 10 AM, pretty much working all day. Then I had five days free in Santa Cruz, until Friday. Since the turnaround time in San Jose was eight hours exactly, and it took forty-five minutes to drive over the mountain to Santa Cruz, while I was working I could get only five hours of sleep if I came home. So I either slept between runs on my conductor's couch, in the back of my truck, or in a switchman's shanty in San Jose. Add in my Saturday date in the city and, on Sundays, I was sleepwalking through my double, very aware of the humiliation of a physical job when you are just bone tired.

Dating Veronica was like meeting a true counterpart, someone from an alternate universe that occupied the same territory as mine. "Cops go everywhere," she told me, "from roach-infested crack houses to mansions on Nob Hill." They could certainly park everywhere, which in San Francisco was an amazing perk. Knowledge

is a problem, though, because once you have it, you can't get rid of it. Veronica knew too much about the place, what crimes had happened there, right where you were having lunch. Off duty, she always packed a gun. "Just in case some guy sees a woman and thinks he can get away with it," she said. I wasn't sure if it made me feel safer or not. The railroad, I realized, lent itself to daydreaming out of time in a way police work did not. The railroad, after all, was just a corridor for moving freight or passengers. Freight work especially took you to back-door places, but you were in and out of them quickly. You didn't have to get up close and personal, the way cops did.

One time Veronica and her partner, Harry, also gay, were working as decoys on the 22 Filmore bus, a particularly rowdy route. A street guy sat down next to her.

"You look like you might like the women," he said. "Is that what you like? Getting nasty with the women?"

Harry was standing up in the row behind them now.

"So what are you going to do about it, you fat faggot?" the guy said.

Throwing him on the floor and dragging him off the bus was a particularly sweet arrest that day.

The one time we went out and she couldn't wear her gun was a formal event we were in gowns and heels for. In the elevator on the way up to the party, a scruffy-looking guy got on pushing a buddy in a wheelchair. Hairy, Viet Nam–era old, tattoos, the jail kind. I could see Veronica turning apoplectic. He was closest to me, in my great aunt's black crocheted gown, and eyeball to eyeball he said, "What if I was to throw you off the roof?" I held his gaze and said, "Oh, I don't think so." I feared for his life, I really did. The door opened and he and his buddy went through it.

I turned to Veronica. "Well, what was your plan?"

"My high heels," she said. "I was going to put one through his eyeball."

Since we essentially had a twelve-hours-a-week relationship, Veronica invented various parlor games for us to play, using the city as a backdrop. One Saturday I received instructions to dress up and take a cab to a specified address. I was instructed not to wear underwear. Not a problem since I was from southern California and the only reason I did wear underwear was to survive in my commute passenger suit. But no matter. Let the revels begin. In a rather femme outfit, I gave the cabdriver the address. He let me out on top of Nob Hill at the Hotel Huntington. A doorman quickly ushered me inside. The destination had to be the Big Four Bar, gleaming like the millionaire's private car it simulated, named for Huntington, Crocker, Stanford, and Hopkins, the founders of the Southern Pacific Railroad. Cozy green leather banquettes fronted round wood tables appointed with brass lanterns. Railroad memorabilia from the early Southern Pacific days hung on the paneled walls. Veronica was sitting at a table, looking as if she had stepped out of one of the pictures. Her jet hair and velvet jacket framed her translucent skin and dark Italian eyes. Only a woman could have thought of this.

"Why the special instructions?" I said.

"I just want to know you are naked under your dress." Women know about getting in the mood.

We had salads in the Big Four Restaurant and as we left the hotel, I noticed that her car was parked on the corner sidewalk. It was like having a valet, in the person of the city itself. She was showing me the breadth of her world. Throwing her ticket book, which had been marking the windshield, into the back seat, Veronica drove me to her flat, a clean, decent place in the Potrero Hill district she had lovingly renovated piece by piece. She was currently working on the curved wooden balustrades for her stairs. It meant a lot to her to fix the place up, since she hadn't been able to do much with the surrounding neighborhood. Feathering a nest was something that the railroad had withheld from me. I had tried to hold on to my cabin in the Santa Cruz Mountains, but my bad seniority had thrown me all around the railroad system, from Santa Cruz to Texas. Eventually, all I had was the dream of a home, something I wrote about.

Some time later, between the sheets, I noticed the time. 10:30—time to get back to the train. Veronica's dog Lucy the Rottweiler was busy licking us whenever we got too close to the edge of the bed.

"I'd love to come with you sometime," Veronica said, holding Lucy at bay while slobber dripped down her arm.

"Why don't you come with me tonight?" I heard myself saying. At the moment it seemed like a golden continuation of a casino winning streak. Everything had been going so smoothly.

"OK," she said, leaping out of bed. For a moment I saw the Salinas teenager she must have been before she knew all about choke holds.

Leaving Salinas, for Veronica, meant escaping the domineering Italian father who used to throw her around. But she also told me about her grandmother, who wore a babushka and hid forbidden *bacalao* behind the refrigerator.

"You could smell it in the house," she said, "and it would drive my father crazy."

It all made the job, and the gun, a little more understandable.

The change room at 4th and Townsend was deserted, just grimy tables littered with playing cards and newspapers. The sprung bunks in the back room where trainmen slept between runs were empty too. No trains here until the morning commute. I met Larry my conductor on the platform and introduced Veronica. I told him I wouldn't be crashing on his couch tonight.

"Just hatcheck her seat and highball us out," he said, giving me a conspiratorial look. Larry was a major poonhound.

I highballed us out of the city at midnight and started up from the rear punching tickets and assessing the drunks. The midnight train was the last resort for people who shouldn't be behind the wheel: Japanese businessmen with briefcases padlocked to their wrists and barely able to hold on to the poles in the middle of the cars, Peninsula society people out on the town with tickets for Menlo Park, rowdy out-of-towners headed for cheaper hotels. We seemed to have a particularly inebriated train tonight, including a bunch of men in baseball caps, singing noisily. At Bayshore, I opened the doors to let passengers off and as I was about to highball the engineer to leave, I noticed a stream of liquid shooting out in an arc from an open door up the train.

"Goddamit," I thought. "I'm not closing the door on that. Guess who gets to stand in that stairwell?" I picked up my radio. "Larry, got some pissers in the third car. I think that's your specialty." Just last week, when a supervisor from the Joint Powers Commission, which was about to take over Caltrain operations, was riding with us, some very drunk person had taken off all his clothes. When Larry confronted him, the man actually swung his penis in a circle at him, while sticking his tongue out. "Wow," I thought, "men actually do that." The supervisor was in the car at the time, looking at the floor. "I bet he really wants this operation now," I thought.

We had to call ahead to the cops and have him dragged off, still naked, at Sunnyvale. I hoped Veronica was not going to get an eyeful tonight. She wasn't, after all, working. Instead, she got to see a very well-dressed woman throw up on her own shoes in the vestibule between the cars—on her shoes and on the hand brake, which I would be operating later that night. Someone else, meanwhile, was letting go all over one of the seat cushions. This was karmic punishment,

I felt, for all my hippie carousing years. At least I was paying it off.

Finally, we arrived in San Jose at 1:30 and could get off the vomitorium. As we wended our way into the passenger yard, I could see the homeless tucked away in their improvised tents under the switch stands and rolled in cardboard in the dark corners of the terminal. Sleeping sometimes as I did in my truck or in the shanty, I felt only the thinnest separation between us. The switchman's joke, "See that guy there? He used to be a good engineer," held a truth nobody wanted to acknowledge. My job and a piece of plastic in my wallet were the only difference. Here I was at 1:30 in the morning, looking for shelter.

"OK," I said brightly as I escorted Veronica to my truck, "let's see what's open."

That turned out to be the San Jose Inn, a railroad motel I knew from the union meetings held there. The night clerk checked us in with only minimal scrutiny and at 2 AM we settled in to much-deserved sleep. For about thirty minutes. At 3:00 a block party erupted in the room next to us and continued nonstop for the next two hours. Veronica was getting that ballistic look. She probably did have her gun with her. I decided to get us a new room before she decided she had to solve the problem.

"Sorry," the desk clerk said. "It's prom night."

"Prom night at the San Jose Inn?" I thought. "Good Lord."

Our new room, the last one at the back of the motel, was mercifully quiet and we settled in to get our three hours sleep until I was on duty for the morning run back. Same equipment as the night before, only now cooking in its own stew. Still, we had come to rest, found a soft pillow and a locked door. Found peace. In the morning, Veronica got up, said, "Well, it's a new day," and opened the door to let a little Sunday sunlight in. The first sight she saw was someone crawling out of a Goodwill dumpster on the corner. First class all the way.

I found us coffee and food and drove us back to the depot to air test our train, but the absurdities of the night before hovered around us like laughing baboons. The Big Four Bar had been half of a picture trying to complete itself. The Nob Hill mansion required the careening drunks, the tracks through funky parts of town, the midnight hours, the dead-tired workers, the seedy railroad motel at the end of the line, and the dumpster denizen in morning's light, to remind us of what true desperation looks like, what Big Four wealth creates. The spirit of the railroad would not let Nob Hill stand alone, without a qualifier. From "don't wear underpants" to *sans culottes*. The whole enchilada. Veronica looked at me, tying the brake with gloves on to avoid Palo Alto debutante puke.

"Well," she said, smiling, "it was real."

YARD JOB. COLTON, CALIFORNIA.

The Southern Pacific Railroad, for my whole career, was trying to dismantle itself. Over half the roster disappeared. Technology changed the craft radically. There were mileposts in this process; in 1984 we lost the caboose and one brakeman on a crew. Eight years later, the other brakeman was in jeopardy. The company wanted to run trains with just a conductor and an engineer. This was part of an overall trend away from local freight to long-haul port to destination runs. The company opened with a sweet deal, which was temporary—a buyout only the oldest heads could take and an offer of half pay to stay home on a reserve board, subject to a twenty-eight-day recall. Most people couldn't survive on half pay, unless they had a second job, which was an old tradition on the railroad, but California mortgages left most people needing the full paycheck. Half pay, however, was pretty close to what I was making anyway, with our trainmaster assiduously cutting me off every weekend and most of the winter. And so, while the union hashed the contract out with the company, always a bad news process for us, I decided to bid in the reserve board and try to accomplish something else in my life, namely learning Spanish. Growing up in LA, I had always known how important it was, and working on the railroad in the Southwest had brought that knowledge home to me. The immigrants on our train, the bilingualism of place names and California history—it all reached a point where I could no longer stay ignorant.

In February of 1992, I won the reserve board and went to Oaxaca, Mexico, for six weeks to live with a family and study in a language school. I learned about the school from my friend Barbara, who was selling stuff at the flea market one weekend. She had a rain stick from Mexico and shook it while she told me about the school in Oaxaca. It was a turning point in my life. I called the family's phone number given me by the school and couldn't understand a word spoken by whomever had answered. Luckily, I had a street address. I rang the doorbell and Guadalupe Pedroarona de Pisano, accompanied by a young indigenous maid, answered the door. It was as if the person I had cared the most for in my life, my own grandmother who died when I was 7, had come back to life. The resemblance was that strong. Neither of us understood a word, but the body language said everything. Lupita hugged me like family and showed me to my room, up the narrowest of stairs, all open to the air, to a small room with an ancient single bed, a mattress as old as the revolution, and a 20-foot ceiling. There were three such rooms on this floor and an iron gate that led to the rooftop where you hung laundry and could watch the street below.

To learn a language, you have to have the consciousness of a child, and the coincidence of the grandmother made it possible for me to be a child again in Mexico. I now have a Mexican personality, which only exists when I speak Spanish, formed primarily by Lupita, who cooked for me every day and treated me like an adopted child. I speak the way this family speaks and I learned about Mexican culture at their table. Lupita had seven daughters and one of them, Elda, who was my age, had chosen not to marry, to have a career teaching, and to stay home with her mother. Lupita had also never been alone a minute in her whole life. Even if going to the market, she always was accompanied. I thought about my life on the railroad. There was no way she was going to understand anything about it. Even my wanderings around town were probably mystifying to her. Why would I go alone? And so I let this family wrap me into itself and I heard its gossip and greeted its members as they came in and out of the family house for extended visits. I was the mascot, their North American. Soon everyone on the street knew who I was and where I belonged. Oaxaca was now completely safe for me.

When I came home at the end of March, I could enroll in my local junior college's intensive Spanish 3 with no difficulties. Since summer was our busy time, I was back working until the fall when I won the reserve board again and could take intensive Spanish 4. Winter 1993, I won the board again and went back to Oaxaca for three months, lived with the same family and studied privately with my former teacher.

They say that moving into fluency is like a window shade rolling up all of a sudden. It was like that. I began to dream in Spanish. I could speak whole sentences. I began to have Mexican friends.

My old friend Barbara had met Yvonne in Oaxaca years before, when she was having trouble finding a seat in a restaurant in the *zocalo,* the town center. Yvonne had invited her to sit down with her and her boyfriend, and Barbara won them over. Their family had been scandalized, Yvonne later told her. Yvonne's father, a doctor in Tehuantepec, later told me he had been surprised that Barbara was so old (around 60 at the time). An unlikely friend for Yvonne, who was about 20, but then Barbara had this magnetic quality that drew people and she could communicate heart to heart and have long conversations in Spanish, even though she didn't really speak it. She

had the widest variety of friends, from waiters to teachers to poets to singers. I, on the other hand, wanted to speak grammatically and found it much harder to meet people. So I borrowed friends from Barbara, Yvonne among them.

During crazy February (*Febrero loco y en Mars un otro poco,* crazy February and in March another little bit), Yvonne invited me to Tehuantepec to visit her family. She couldn't leave until early morning, so I went down on my own, a four-hour bus ride south to the isthmus. My Mexican family warned me about going. Oaxacans were sure that people living elsewhere in Mexico were backward.

"The people there are dirty and lazy," they said. "And there are thieves on the road."

I knew this was true because I had started reading the papers. Bandits, often in collusion with bus drivers, put tires across the highway in remote locations and robbed night buses.

I asked Yvonne if she was afraid of bandits.

"Oh yes," she said, "but I'm Catholic and I pray to the virgin."

So when I got on the bus, I prayed to the virgin and said, "Look, I'm not Catholic, but everyone else on this bus is, so don't let us get robbed."

The road wound and wound in the dark, always downward. We descended 5,000 feet until the land evened out a little and we crossed a big river that wasn't cascades but slow moving. The moon was full and I had a window seat, so I could see a train paralleling our road. It seemed to go under us and re-emerge alongside, like an articulated dragon, but for me it was a welcome friend. Later, in an art gallery in Oaxaca, I saw a painting of this train, in the form of a sea serpent diving and surfacing into a salty lagoon. The artist was from Tehuantepec.

The railroad ran directly in front of Yvonne's family home—so close that, if there were a derailment, the train would land in their living room. Her father walked me there from the humid bus station, where I got off at 2 AM and didn't know a soul. They put me in their only bed. Everyone else slept in hammocks in the other rooms, nobody but me noticing the Japanese clock that rang every hour with a different song. Yvonne arrived sometime during the night, and in the morning we put plastic chairs in the back of their pickup truck and rode past coconut palms and mango groves to a natural spring where we swam while majestic women in long skirts served sweet bread and coconuts with straws.

"Oro de Tehuantepec," Yvonne's father said, noticing me drinking a coconut. "Now you will always return."

Looking at my passport, I can see he was right. I have returned to Mexico every year, sometimes more. Before we caught the bus back to Oaxaca, the family pulled out a gift they wanted me to take back to the States, an alabaster desk ornament of two stone owls separated by pen holders. It must have weighed 50 pounds. It reminded me of Mussolini's "typewriter" statue in Rome. Inscribed in stone at its base was the name Leon Panetta. He was our congressman in Santa Cruz. Why did this family in Tehuantepec want to give him stone owls?

Barbara's hospitality was the cause. When she met Yvonne years before, she invited her and her mother to visit in the States. Barbara had to go to Leon Panetta to get the necessary juice to bring these middle-class Mexicans to the United States. Now this was the gift in return. Looking around their house, there wasn't much evidence of affluence. Owls are the traditional symbol for lawyers, the course of study Yvonne was pursuing in Oaxaca. It was possible that Panetta was getting a diverted gift for Yvonne, but obligations had to be repaid. My reception was probably part of it all. Unfortunately, I was planning on traveling to Guatemala and I could not carry this cargo with me, so I reluctantly refused. They didn't seem fazed. They were absolutely certain that Leon Panetta would get this owl and if it wasn't now then it would be sometime in the future. I thought this belief was really Mexican, the quality that made daily life in Mexico so positive.

While Barbara and I were perfectly free to come visit Mexico, the opposite was not true. Congressional intervention for a two-week visit? Most of my Mexican friends, who were not doctors or professionals, could never get a visa. They had to have $2,000 in a bank account in their name. And even if they did, it would mean an all-day wait in a line at the embassy in Mexico City. More expenses for travel to the capital, a hotel, eating out. No wonder North Americans seemed oblivious to them, on their beach vacations. The border gate swung only one way.

I saw what the riders on our desert trains were leaving behind. Beauty, family, culture, but no work. No irrigation for agriculture. No potable water. No ability to better yourself through education. North American thirst for drugs ruining any chance of a good government. I spoke to Lizbeth, another of Barbara's young friends, whose musician husband was feeling the pull of the border. She valued what they had in Oaxaca. He saw its limitations. To me, it seemed like they would lose a lot if they came to the States. He sang opera in a sixteenth-century school building. She wrote poetry. In the United States they would be "illegals." Here they had dignity. But here they would always work to just get by. Perhaps in places where the culture was not so strong, it would be easier to leave, but I realized that for most undocumented immigrants, the necessity to leave had a tragic dimension.

Coming from the workaholic U.S. culture, what Mexico taught me was how to live without being obsessed by money. Since access to power was beyond most anyone's grasp, Mexicans concentrated on what they could enjoy now. Interactions with people were very important, and even the smallest interchange was polite. Personal dignity, even of street beggars, was respected. Losing your cool was unheard of. For North Americans, the smallest inconvenience was enough to send them into a rage. For Mexicans, it took election fraud or military violence. Within the protected cloud of normal life, however, this was truly a polite society, anchored by the weight of the family, primarily the women.

Barbara later told me about how the owl got to the United States.

"So, ultimately my doctor released me to travel in Mexico again and I went to Tehuantepec one more time and here is the owl with Leon Panetta's name on it and they wanted me to bring it back and I said, 'It's too heavy, I can't take it,' and they said, 'Leon Panetta has to have it and we went to a great deal of expense to have this made for him and you have to help us get it to the United States.' So I carried this 50-pound owl back to Oaxaca, carried it on the plane because I was afraid to ship it, had to change planes in Mexico City, carried it around all day and finally put it on the second plane."

Of course, when she finally got it to the United States, Leon Panetta was in Washington, D.C., and he couldn't accept gifts. But it will get to him eventually, if God wills it.

With my Spanish under my belt, I crossed the southern border to Guatemala and traveled by second-class bus. It was April and time to bid in the reserve board again. I won it, but our perverse trainmaster called me back to work anyway. It was a long way to go, but I returned home and marked up. I felt like a tooth that had just been extracted. Now I was a railroader again. But after three weeks with no work, the trainmaster cut me off, no doubt figuring he could resume his weekend call backs and I would be so desperate I would take them, thereby getting around our guarantee for protecting the extra board twenty-four hours a day, seven days a week. So in June I transferred to the San Francisco extra board, where I would have to drive for an hour and a half to take any calls. In July I tried Watsonville again, but bounced back and forth between San Francisco, Oakland, and Watsonville for the rest of the year. Being the baby, I could never say my situation was discrimination, but I'm sure the trainmaster got a kick out of cutting me off and watching me scramble for the work. And scramble I did. Only now, like Caliban, I was cursing him in Spanish: *puta madre pinche cabron!*

SHEEP FENCE AND TRAIN. COLGATE SIDING, MONTANA.

On January 1, 1994, the Zapatistas came out of the Lancandon jungle and took over the town of San Cristobal de las Casas, where I had been visiting two weeks before. I wished I could be there, instead of where I was, facing the Southern Pacific's implementation of the region/system board. Management had decided to utilize their surplus brakemen on the airline system and have a roster of extra crew members who could be deployed anywhere for twenty days at a time, then flown back home for ten days. This system sounds efficient in principle, but there are differences between crewing on a railroad versus an airline. In the air, the territory is the same. If you are serving coffee from Seattle to LA, it is just like serving coffee from New York to Boston. On the railroad, the entire track is unique and knowledge of the territory is 90 percent of the job. A typical large switching yard has hundreds of tracks whose numbers may or may not still be on their respective track switches. Track maps are usually out of date. Locals don't want to share information, particularly with boomers they regard as interlopers on the dole. After a minimum of fifteen years on the job, we were all good help, but the work was going to be frustrating and slow, not to mention dangerous, if we went to a different terminal each month.

I had been a boomer before, my first years on the railroad when I was cut off in my home terminal every winter. But that travel was voluntary and on my own dime. Being forced to leave home was something else.

And what about Boomer, my cat? What was she going to do for twenty days while I was gone? I complained to Kevin Klein, my union general chairman, that this new system was woman-unfriendly. Men usually had someone keeping the home together for them while they went on the road.

"It's the same for everybody," he said.

"What railroad woman that you know has someone at home keeping things together?"

"Well, that doesn't prove anything," he said.

So I put my stuff in storage and moved into my friend Donna's spare room. A coyote had carried off her cat and she was fond of Boomer. I bought a trundle bed that barely fit into the tiny space. It felt like a regression into childhood. But I had to streamline. I couldn't leave town for all that time each month and have bills to pay, an animal to feed, and messages to retrieve. I would be grabbing a duffle and living out of a suitcase most of the month. It started in January in Roseville, a hump yard at the foot of the Sierra Nevada.

The hotel room in Roseville had a TV in every room, including the bathroom. This was supposed to be upscale. Outside it was raining and cold. Roseville had an unfortunate climate—105 degrees in summer, cold as hell in winter. I had worked into it before as a brakeman from Dunsmuir to the north and Oakland to the south. I at least knew the layout of the yard. As in the LA yard, crews in Roseville did parts of moves. There were lots of crews working both ends at the same time. The winter Olympics were on TV most of the time I was there, and I tried to think of my stint as an athletic feat and not just trudging around lost in the mud. That idea vanished when I woke up the next morning with a fever and sinus infection. My first feeling was dread—how could I work feeling like this? Then the reflex of blaming myself kicked in. As if I could be a machine totally at the disposition of the railroad. How dare the machine break down? I was conditioned to feel this. The railroad really wanted machines doing the work, not people, and they treated us as machines. I knew the crew dispatcher was going to give me a hard time about laying off. Since I was on a twenty-day stand, I didn't know if I even could lay off. I didn't know a doctor there anyway. But sinus infections could last a month if I didn't get on them right away. I called the crew dispatcher.

"We don't send you there to lay off," he said.

"No shit," I said. Then I went looking for a doc in the box. Some serious antibiotics later, I fell asleep watching downhill racing and listening to it rain. Not an auspicious beginning to life on the road this time around.

Still determined to figure it out, in spite of the fact that I knew in my bones this renewed booming was not going to work for me, I bought a fold-up bike from a big RV store catering to the camping retired crowd, as opposed to the camping hobo crowd that inhabited Roseville's outskirts. I thought that if they sent me far afield, I could always take it on the plane and still have some transportation wherever I went.

On my last shift in Roseville, the top end herder kept making mistake after mistake, but everyone was nice to him anyway. One of the switchmen told me, "It's a shame he has to be working out here. He's come back from cancer and has to be pounding the lead." I just thought, "Well, he had insurance. Why isn't he at home?"

What was I feeling that month in Roseville? Fear that this new dislocation meant that I would never have a home. Worry that I couldn't keep living this way. I had quit drinking, come home to Santa Cruz, and vowed not to go booming, but the railroad wouldn't let me stay. My seniority wouldn't let me. My cabin up in the mountains had been too remote to work an extra board from, so I sold it to a dope dealer who was raising magic mushrooms in the basement. Home prices in town were beyond me, and more than that, I was never sure I could work here in peace. The ferret trainmaster was always cutting me off the board in Watsonville, and even San Francisco or Oakland was beyond my seniority. I would have to move to LA to be sure of a job, and I had come from LA. I wasn't moving back. Being who I was, I couldn't let myself sign up for a huge mortgage for a house I couldn't live in while I chased my job around the Southwest. I needed to keep things simpler than that. So first I rented, and now here I was, moving in with a friend and sleeping in a trundle bed while the railroad signed me up for what seemed to be an impossible task. When was this ever going to end? The problem was, the railroad always offered a panoramic view of the abyss, populated by the homeless we shared the railroad space with.

The archetype of the view was in El Paso, Texas, where I was headed on the board next month. Ten years before, when I went booming on my own dime, El Paso was where I had ended up. There you could look out your apartment window and see true desperation in the dark hillsides covered with cardboard shanties. I was just getting sober then, and El Paso was literally the end of my rope, as far away from California as my system seniority would take me. There I met other kindred spirits who were running away, one of whom was Al, who ended up being my roommate. We lived together as friends trying to stay sober, or in his case, trying to stay clean. I know Al never denied the rumors that we were lovers, and I didn't either. Not that he needed the rep. Women found him irresistible, the dark slim good looks, his vulnerability. He told me one time some home guard hoghead asked him what I was like in bed. Al said he asked him, "Well, what's your wife like in bed?" He had this innate courtesy. Sleaziness like that really did offend him.

Al's troubles with drugs dated to Viet Nam. He used to say that in El Paso pushers were always able to spot him for a user, wherever he went. In the grocery store or a gas station, he always heard *"chiva"* whispered. It would be like my trying to stay sober in Napa Valley. I was in El Paso because there weren't any wineries, but there sure were drugs. Our apartment faced the green ribbon of the Rio Grande, which immigrants waded over constantly. I guess it was a view of how we could be worse off than we were and a reminder of how far there was to fall. Our place was also very close to the treatment center Al went into after he met me and decided to get sober. Our place was his halfway house and my first sober home, since I had been on the run ever since I sobered up in Santa Cruz a year before. I know I was his prop, but any external support was a house of cards and only temporary, since all your cards had to fall on you before you could really get out and start building.

At meetings in El Paso, Al was running into the AA snobbery of alcohol vs. drug addiction. Baby boomers usually were cross-addicted—Viet Nam vets with smack, everybody else with grass or pills. I couldn't understand the Bohemian Club attitude. So being a drunk was high class? I know that when I was snorting coke and smoking grass, I didn't even consider alcohol a drug, until I woke up one morning an alcoholic. I think Al was still there with alcohol. Compared to smack, it didn't seem like a big problem. Drugs were illegal, and if you were high, you had to think twice about being a good citizen. Particularly on the railroad, where alcoholism was practically a religion, but drug users were regarded as scum.

I stayed in El Paso, riding trains into the desert, until I thought I could face California and its good-life wine culture again. Packing to go home, I had to throw out a lid of pot I had been saving "just in case," all that time. It was my reservation. You can't have any of those. Al stayed on. Like Lawrence of Arabia, there was only the desert for him.

When I left El Paso, I temporarily moved in with Margo in Oakland for a few months, to work out of there. One morning I went outside to find a note from Al on my windshield. He had come and gone in the night. Another time, he visited me when I got a place in Santa Cruz in 1986, leaving a deer haunch in my freezer. I always knew we'd shared something we both valued, living on the border.

I think it was my first year back in California that I heard about the overdose. Al had been going to Narcotics Anonymous because he didn't think alcohol was his problem. I can understand that with a heroin problem, alcohol seems like maintenance, but to get clean and sober you couldn't do it your way, deciding what the problem was and what wasn't. You had no idea what the problem was and wouldn't for years. You just had to trust. Anyway, meetings were a good place to meet women and a good place to meet people who liked to get high, and after a meeting Al and a woman scored some dope and she overdosed. There he was alone with a dead person. He panicked. There's a lot of desert around El Paso and Al drove her out into it and buried her.

They tell you in the program not to get involved with anyone the first year sober. I thought, probably like most people, that the old heads were just killjoys. No booze, no drugs, now no sex. I didn't get it that they were warning you for your life. Well, now I got it. The relationship Al and I had, looking out for each other's sobriety, was the model for love. You wanted the best for the other person, whether it was about you or not. Picking up someone for sex, taking the edge off whatever withdrawal was making you uncomfortable, was not. And it was doubly dangerous because you had an accomplice.

Coming from Viet Nam, though, Al's standard for craziness and danger was probably very askew. The freedom the railroad offered to lead double and triple lives was very tempting. If you got into trouble, you just made a seniority move somewhere else. Al told me he showed the steps of the program to a solid citizen type on the railroad, and the guy told him, "You know, these are just common-sense things that most normal people live by." Well, for us, they weren't intuitive. As a matter of fact, you had to override nearly every impulse you had in early sobriety. It was guaranteed to be wrong.

Going to El Paso again, I was sure that railroad gossip would throw this story in my face. As they say, telephone, telegraph, tell a rail. Sure enough, as soon as I walked into the switchman's shanty, an old head ran right over to tell me the decade-old news.

"You know that guy you were livin' with, that boomer. Well, he buried his girlfriend!"

What could I say? It was true. Offer that she was, after all, dead? And that she had made the choice that got her that way? If she had drunk twenty shooters and overdosed on alcohol, why wouldn't that have been as bad? Of course, then Al wouldn't have had the problem of his own addiction; he wouldn't have had to cover his own ass first by dumping her.

Even though he came from a railroad family and the railroad would forgive a lot, this was too much. Al never gave me the details of losing his job, but suddenly he was still in El Paso, but he wasn't working for the railroad anymore. I would later find out it took him a year and a lawsuit to get back on. He was unconvincingly optimistic on the phone.

"So Al, how's it going, then?"

"Oh it's going great, really. I got a house out in the desert with another boomer."

"Well, how's the money thing, then?"

"Oh well, you can get over $25 for a rattlesnake skin, and evenings out at Alfalfa yard, you find 'em all over there. That idiot moved a few of them onto our porch, though; I've got to talk to him about that shit."

I had thought that the overdose was about as bottomed out as it could get, but in the surreal landscape surrounding El Paso at that time, one death was like a grain of dust. Bodies of female *maquilladora* workers would amass there and become as ordinary as road kill. When my friend Leslie heard the story, she said, knowingly, "Ah, he became a rattlesnake hunter." In her cosmology, such hunters were sorcerers who had moved over to the dark side. Later, traveling in northern Mexico, I would see the roadside stands where rattlesnake skins hung in the desert like scalps.

I heard stories about other boomers who stayed behind. One of them was found in a motel room outside Lordsburg, tied to a chair and shot in the back of the head. There was something about the desert there that was like the edge of the civilized world. You could escape into it, but you brought your ghosts with you. It sobered you up or it killed you. Al's story haunted me because I loved him and worried for myself. We were trying to walk the same road. Was my version of this story still waiting for me somewhere? As my friend Linda the Buddhist put it, "We all wonder, how far will we go? Even if it's just eating donuts at work. Will I weigh 300 pounds? Do all journeys end in a desert with a dead body in your trunk?" Some friends of hers had dropped LSD and were walking around in Death Valley in California. They came upon a body lying on the sand. After panicking about being high themselves, they drove to a pay phone and reported it. Two weeks later, sober, they returned to the same spot, and the body was still there.

There was something else. By getting sober, I had to face one great denial in my life. But denial didn't end there. In the summer, I had a routine breast exam at my doctor's office. Actually she was a new doc I was seeing and she called my attention to a lump in my breast.

"How long has this been here?" she asked.

"Well, I get regular mammograms and exams, so I guess it's new," I said.

"Well, I want to watch it," she said.

Now I didn't consciously bury that idea and I don't remember thinking that it was something I had to put off dealing with until my railroad life became more stable. But I now know that is what my unconsciousness decided. I was moving out of my home and the railroad was sending me booming again. "One thing at a time," I thought. And then I didn't think about it again.

ORDER BOARD. IOWA FALLS, IOWA.

Since I had worked in El Paso before, a year in 1984, I could actually do my job when the railroad sent me there in March. And I had old friends. What had changed was that I now spoke Spanish. This to them was an event more incredible than if I had gone to the moon.

"*Sí, hijo de la chingada,*" my foreman said as an aside, while on the phone with the yardmaster.

"*Cuidate, entiendo todo,*" I said, watching his jaw drop.

I was there ten years earlier and I didn't speak Spanish. Now I did. How could that happen?

"You just learned Spanish? Nobody does that."

All I can say is that the border culture is entrenched and each side is resisting and assimilating the other. This time, though, the language opened the border to me and I heard the stories, as numerous as desert trails.

I was sitting in the company motel coffee shop between eight-on eight-off shifts in the yard, talking to a friendly New Mexican down from San Jon. J.D. was a sunny guy, blonde hair, blue eyes, with a kind of cowboy aura about him. He seemed innocent, as if he lived in the world of the cowboy mural of ghost riders painted along the main drag of San Jon, something I had driven out from Tucumcari to photograph in 1983.

"Oh, that," J.D. said. "It's gone now. They painted it over."

The cowboy mural wasn't all that was gone. A new presence was on the border now; it had gone corporate in a big way. Like magnets, huge *maquilladora* factories lined the border, "finishing" American products and evading American pollution and labor laws. They attracted young workers, mostly women, from all over Mexico, who moved to the border and lived in sprawling cardboard *colonias* without sanitation, water, or adequate transportation. The turnover was 100 percent, but central Mexico had wave on wave of workers to send north. The men crossed over and rode our trains to the north; the women worked the factories.

J.D. had been out drinking in a singles bar and met a man with a story. There was something compulsive about it; when you heard it you needed to tell it to someone else, maybe to figure out what had hooked you.

"This guy Bud," J.D. said, "is sleazy looking. Ostrich boots, wrong hair, young but women wouldn't like him. He's trying too hard. He don't fit his jeans. Kind of guy looking for a fast score, easy money. But doesn't have the guts to be an outlaw. Try to lay you on the first date, 'cause he knows you ain't comin' back for no second date. Well, he meets a man in a bar. The guy recruited him. Needed a manager, a white man, to oversee a plant in Juarez. Someone who spoke Mexican and could run things.

"'It's a different deal over there,' the man told him. 'You run your own show, just so you produce. Are we on the same page, Bud?'"

So Bud got a new suit and a moustache trim and drove across the Freedom Bridge to Juarez.

"The workers are all young girls," J.D. told me. "All about 16. They only stay a couple of years; they work 'em so hard."

Bud had clearly filled him in about this point. He kept repeating it.

"They give 'em sandwiches for lunch and lemonade, but they water that down. If they come in late one time, they're gone. Their boyfriends meet them in the parking lot and beat 'em up and take their money. They really work 'em hard."

Bud, the manager, had an aerial view of the workers, perched in an office on an open second floor. Railroad managers often acted like boys with keys to their father's Porsche, but this temptation was of a different order.

A divide was opening up between J.D. and me. Because I was "one of the boys," railroaders respected my work. But they went to strip joints, paid for lap dances, and badmouthed the Mexican women working there.

"You're the one paying them," I'd say. "They wouldn't be working there if you weren't employing them."

"Well, you don't do that kind of work," they'd say.

"I don't have to," I'd say. "I'm one of the 1 percent of women who can have this kind of job."

Case in point was the *maquilla* workers. They were women. They were workers. But still, there was this sexual greediness surrounding them, and soon much worse than that. In 2001, one worker, age 20, was four minutes late for work at an assembly plant and got shut out. She tried to return home but never made it. She joined the 450 women murdered in Juarez since 1983.

"They live in those *colonias* way out of town," J.D. told me. "They can't afford to live in Juarez. Sometimes they have to change buses four times, and to get home and back, sometimes it isn't worth it, so they sleep in cardboard near to the *maquilla*."

I, of course, had done much the same thing to work on the railroad. The back of my truck was my second home.

"They can't be late or they get fired. And you know, they spend their money dressing up. They come to work dressed like it's a date—high heels, short skirts, makeup and all. They look like they're going to a high-school prom."

That fact rang true to me. It seemed there was no middle ground in the way Mexican women dressed. The indigenous women were modest in the extreme, but to work in the modern culture, they assumed their function was to appear sexy. Of course young factory women would dress that way. Other than the Zapatista female commanders, just coming out of the jungle in 1994, there were few models for independent working women who weren't hyper-feminine.

The Maya in Mexico have stories about the Earth Lord, who controls all wealth and lives in a cave under the mountain. He dresses like those in power, wearing a cowboy hat and pointy boots. Now he probably wears a suit and tassel loafers. He demands his due, before he will surrender money.

Listening to J.D., I felt polluted somehow. Who did he think I was in the story? I had to be the female worker, since I couldn't be the manager. Although we both worked on the railroad, I would never get that particular invitation, to be the boss of a *maquilladora*. Of course, I was also the U.S. consumer who bought the goods the women slaved over. A double whammy.

"He's going to take me over there," J.D. told me. "So I can see the whole thing. Aren't you interested? I mean, who wouldn't be interested in a story like that?"

It was Bud's need for a confidant that had me interested. Another *Picture of Dorian Gray*. A hormone-pumped Bud on the Juarez side, hustling teenage workers and driving a sports car, while the El Paso Bud became ever more grotesque and untouchable. American women drifted away whenever he explained what he did. He found himself drinking more, seeking a confidant, a convert, like J.D. His own mother, J.D. told me, came to see him, and looking at the guard tower office perched over the factory floor, said, "Can't you find something decent to do with your life?"

Decent was a luxury there, the luxury of sixteen-hour workdays that actually paid your bills and left you with dirt that would wash off. And yet I could feel J.D.'s story take hold. I wanted to cross the border so I could be the one to tell it. I wished I were a man or were younger or had more courage. The Earth Lord always knows what we want.

DRIVING SPIKES. ELY, NEVADA (WEST OF).

In April, after El Paso, the railroad sent me to work in LA, ironically, my former home. I had left it in 1964 for college, but I only got as far as the University of California, Riverside, about ten miles from the huge West Colton yard that was invisible to me then. In 1967, I transferred up to UC Santa Cruz for my senior year and really never left, marrying a professor and commuting up to graduate school in Berkeley. The LA I left was full of childhood tragedies, the death of my father when I was 17 and the more recent death of my mother. I had a few old friends there, but apart from a few months working in 1979, I had no idea what it had become.

The smog was thick even in April as I drove the five hours down the crystal coast. I knew all the railroad territory into Santa Barbara, as I had worked the Coast Starlight on Amtrak. I had also worked the LA yard when I first hired out in 1979. The hump was gone, now, and what I would be catching would be local freight and short runs from LA to Colton or the City of Industry, a few pool runs up the coast to San Luis Obispo. Local freight jobs went on duty all over the LA metropolitan area. Even though I had grown up in the old rich suburb of Pasadena, I had no idea how to get anywhere the railroad would be sending me, so I asked for a carryall whenever I got a call. It meant longer days, since you were stuck waiting after tying up for some driver to find you, but the papers were full of drive-by shootings and gang wars in the areas we were called to work in.

It was hard to understand the anger I felt being in LA. I can only say that I think I was awake to something new. When I went booming the first time, in 1975, the western states were mysterious and mythical places to me. I was discovering working-class culture, with its pride and prejudices. Drinking made me accepted, but then I had to carve out my own place through sobriety and choices. My story seemed to me to be a story of triumph. I had won sobriety. I had won mastery of my craft. Then, I crossed the border. Learning Spanish in Mexico was like being born again as someone else. In Mexico, I felt connected to the way people lived and worked. They worked their jobs the way I worked mine, only they kept their rootedness. They had a family culture that anchored everything and I felt welcome there, living with a Mexican family. You have to know what something feels like in order to want it in your life, and in Mexico, I was starting to feel at home. This was the place our cross-to-bear trainmaster jerked me back from in May 1993, only to cut me off three weeks later.

Now I looked around me in LA and saw the horror that racism and illegal immigration had created. How did the beauty of Mexican rural culture degenerate into gang culture and violence? It had to come from American culture itself, erasing all that was gentle and beautiful in Mexico. Pushed through the sieve of consumerism, the heliotrope colors milked from seashells onto silk faded in the ozone light. I went to the nearest grocery store and noticed the armed guard in the parking lot. Perhaps I had fled north, years ago, into just a more scenic Pasadena, whose residents felt safe enough to declare their town an immigration sanctuary. Immigrants in Northern California were primarily agricultural workers, but here in LA they worked all the blue-collar jobs. I guess I was getting in touch with the anger at the heart of settled immigrant culture here, in my home, an old anger rooted in the history of the place, an anger I only saw the surface of before. Now I could perceive its roots, the contrast to what that culture could be if nourished. The railroad was making me look at the worst of this. It was placing me right inside it, alone at midnight with a brakeman's lantern, in a concrete roadbed covered with gang graffiti, hearing gunshots and waiting for a red signal that never went green.

It didn't help that the last time I was in Long Beach, here at the port I was switching out, was in 1982 when my sister and I scattered my mother's ashes out to sea. The deranged and addicted homeless dodged our trains as we passed through their living rooms on our nightly rounds. Death and transformation were in the salt air. How long could I hold on to the train before I, too, lost my grip in any of the thousand ways that could happen? Whether an immigrant, a Pasadena housewife, or a young, strong worker in the prime of life.

Luckily, region/system board roulette sent me to West Colton for the next three months, also a scene of desolation but without the existential depth of the City of Angels. West Colton was like a huge prison yard where they paid you. Fittingly, six real prisons and the worst smog in the LA basin surrounded it.

The eight hours drive time from Santa Cruz to Colton consumed the first day on the board, but arriving at 3 PM meant you were rested for the midnight shift, and after that you worked eight-on eight-off around the clock for twenty days. Colton sat up against the San Gabriel Mountains to the east and Mr. San Jacinto to the west, collecting ozone. When I was growing up, citrus groves gave way to date orchards as you entered the Mojave on the other side of the range. Even now its gateway nature hinted of freedom just beyond the perimeter. Through freight came and went, to all the destinations in the West. Despite its ugliness, this scent of the road made it tolerable, that and the absence of the chaos of working LA.

Yard work was routine. There were three shifts a day, and once you mastered the yard, it was just physical activity broken by card games. The heat made it interesting. Your body became who you were. I knew from working Tucson in the summer that overalls and a white cotton T-shirt were the most ventilated clothing. Since I only had eight hours between shifts, laundry was out of the question, and so I left the icy hotel, walked across the connecting elevated passage to the enclosed mall next door, and bought thirty pairs of overalls at Montgomery Ward. A pile of them began to form in my living room, to be taken home in army duffle bags at the end of the stint. Cholo T-shirts with the Virgin of Guadalupe on them, bought at the local flea market, completed my work outfit.

The rhythm of the work became a way of life, and I felt my body growing strong. What I liked about railroad work was having my feet on dirt, not asphalt, tile, concrete, or air, in the case of the hotel room. Living on earth, working on it, breathing it, sweating it out, was what I felt traveling in Mexico. I saw people doing jobs I had done, the ticket collector on the bus, the passenger train conductor, the night freight worker. On the U.S. grid, most people worked inside concrete, air-conditioned, sanitized buildings, watched flat screens, listened to canned music, and talked on cell phones. Watching them in the mall cafés after work, all I could see was their separation and craziness.

In one of these cafés I met a character from one of Leslie's books, *Almanac of the Dead*. The World Cup was in the United States that year and upper-class Mexicans were in our hotel and around town.

"Your character Menardo tried to pick me up yesterday," I told her on the phone.

"Yeah," she said. "He would."

He was explaining his business, how he had to carry large amounts of cash, how he traded anything, lobster, blenders, blue jeans.

"To do business in Mexico," he said, "you have to give parties. It's all who you know. I can buy a boatload of lobster and have a plane loaded with ice by making a phone call. One time, I was robbed in McArthur Park. I have to carry cash. They got $30,000 cash."

In Leslie's book, Menardo trades guns and helicopters and ends up so paranoid he sleeps in his bulletproof vest. This Menardo didn't seem to be wearing one.

On a job at the City of Industry the month before, I felt a desert breeze with released moisture carried up from the Gulf of California, and I suddenly thought, "I should call Leslie." Talking on the phone with her later, she said, "Maybe I was in that wind." She was then getting started on *Gardens in the Dunes*, set right there in Parker Dam and Riverside. Working close to the ground opened up something in me, the perception of distances, how far they actually were, how weather systems traveled them in days, the linking motion of the freight lines and rivers, and how minds time traveled also. I knew from writing that when you travel mentally, a part of you is actually there. Leslie was there through her writing and I had the distinct feeling of her presence.

I remember a shift on the hump, with a switchman named Angel as foreman. He was a Chicano from LA, and we were taking our lunch break at 3 in the morning in the hump shanty, lying on the benches just talking.

"I used to work out, could bench 300 pounds, and shit, you're probably stronger than I am now."

I was strong, from climbing up the sides of high ladders a hundred times a shift, untying brakes, pulling up the cut levers on the hump hundreds of times a night, then resting for eight hours and doing it again. Sweat smelled good, I could feel my clothes molding to my body, skin pumping out the water I poured in, ingesting the air, the dust, and the petroleum railroad dirt. The sun moved across the yard by day, the moon by night. I felt it on my skin, my eyes, where its shadows fell in the yard, how it climbed and descended the framing range, San Gabriels to the east, San Jacinto to the west. In Santiago Atitlan, Guatemala, the guide showed us the altar in the church, with the sun climbing and descending its triptych arch, then took us out the door, which faced the triptych mountains where the sun climbed and descended.

"An altar to the sun," he said.

Switchmen in the yard work an altar to the sun; find the moon refreshing in the summer heat. I thought about how it might feel to be capable of true feats of strength, like Angel, how it would feel to be inside his body, and I realized I could never know.

On one of my trips home, my older sister, who lived in France, came to visit me. On her stateside visits, she tried to keep up with medical things but she was putting off having a biopsy of some calcium deposits in her breast. She had been putting it off for a year. Her solution was to go on a macrobiotic diet. As I listened to her, a bell went off for me. I realized we both were running away from the same thing, so I scheduled a breast exam and the lump was still there. This was at the end of August in my ten days off cycle. Because it was squishy, the doctor wasn't in a huge rush, but we scheduled a biopsy for September, after my twenty days in LA.

The railroad, meanwhile, had moved us out of the squalid Glendale hotel into some yuppie condos in Long Beach, with kitchenette, gym, and pool. At least when you came home grimy and tired, the outside didn't match your inside. The no sleep factor, however, left me feeling like a creature from another world alongside the normal folks by the pool. John Payne was down here also and we explored the upscale beach cafés, almost like lovers on vacation courtesy of the Southern Pacific Railroad. You had to take John on his own terms. He would hole up in his room, and he clearly did not want to be disturbed. When he felt like being social, he would emerge, usually with stories about 400 sit-ups and hours pumping iron. Occasionally, these athletic exercises would go awry, leaving him one time with a detached thumb. Longevity was the key with John. It took a long time to get to know him, but eventually I did.

Depending on the run, I would either drive to Taylor yard in Glendale or to some local yard to catch trains. For any through freight, though, it was safer to go to Glendale, since if you only had eight hours on duty, the railroad would often put you on another train and there was no telling where you would end up. They had to get you back to Taylor yard, eventually. There was so much traffic piling up on sidings trying to get through the LA bottleneck that you would often be called to relieve a crew who had been sidetracked for twelve hours. You would get on their train and you might sit there twelve also, waiting for a green. The yardmaster at Colton wanted trains out of his yard, so he would send them along even if there were no hope of them getting anywhere. They stacked up on every siding between Colton and LA. Sometimes you would be called to work the yard at City of Industry, the halfway point, or to set out trains there and get on other trains.

Conductor-only crews were the rule, just you and an engineer. This made any switching, particularly with long piggybacks or articulated cars, extremely tedious. You had a radio and you shoved into a rail to a joint with what was in there, walked back to the clearance point, cut off what would fit, then shoved into another rail. There was nobody to answer questions if you didn't know the tracks. Just you and the radio.

Other calls were to Compton or Watts at midnight, to switch junkyards, paper houses, or tank farms, the warehouse walls covered with spray can graffiti—all the places I could never have gone, growing up here white and privileged.

Working here, beside the freeways, under palm trees, the San Gabriels as a backdrop, dislocated me in time and space. I was born here. I had seen these mountains and arroyos as a child, ridden them on horseback, breathed in the same air, the same endless summer. I knew the place and I did not. I felt like I had grown up to be someone else.

Toward the end of the month, I was called for a through freight run up the coast to San Luis Obispo, a plum pool job. I couldn't believe some sharpshooter hadn't taken it, but here it was, on duty at 7 PM at Taylor yard.

"We got no work to do, just a straight shot, so kick back and enjoy the ride," the hoghead said.

We knew this was a lucky night. Full moon up the coast, in bed before dawn. Out of Glendale the tracks roller coasted through the San Fernando Valley, the engine echoing off suburban walls, then into the Tehachapi tunnel, a long one that opened out into Oxnard and a straight run along the coast, waves of cane at the Carpenteria trestle, the surf terraced out to sea, its relayed sound, the landscape narrowing before the hobo tree in Santa Barbara, sheltering homeless in the land of the rich, Old Spanish Days notwithstanding. Above Santa Barbara the coast got wild. We passed the small yard at Surf, where I nearly stepped on a rattler one summer night on the Lompoc job. My lantern saw him and I must have flown onto the engine without touching the ground. Lompoc was a job we protected out of Watsonville. It meant a week's stand down there, on duty in the agricultural town of Guadalupe, really a Mexican pueblo since all the workers were migrants. Surf was the gateway to the Vandenburg missile reserve, where rockets went to the moon, their silos surreal sculptures next to Monterey pines and empty dunes, part of the old Hollister Ranch, closed to civilians. Just the train could pass by. In daylight you would see foxes, coyotes, and kites. Then we turned away from the sea, through eucalyptus stripling moonlight. These breaks led us into San Luis, a California mission town, the depot in mission style, the red tiled roofs, the white walls of the village.

The motel was one of my homes. I had worked into San Luis Obispo from Watsonville, knew the town, its croissant and cappuccino mornings. Its Scandinavian whiteness. It was, if anything, too clean. I didn't know it then, but this would be my last main line train, under the jaguar moon, a perfect run.

GALLERY

CONDUCTOR BETWEEN FREIGHT CARS. HETTINGER, NORTH DAKOTA.

BRAKEMAN. SPARKS, NEVADA.

BACK-UP SIGNAL. KNIFE RIVER, NORTH DAKOTA.

MAINTENANCE-OF-WAY WORKER. AMES, IOWA.

MACHINE SHOP
SAFETY FIRST
←1 TRACK 2→

MECHANICS ON BREAK. EAST ELY, NEVADA.

PASSENGER TRAIN. TOPEKA, KANSAS.

ENGINEER SLEEPING.

GALLUP, NEW MEXICO.

RAILROADER HOTEL. FORSYTH, MONTANA.

OFF DUTY. FORSYTH, MONTANA.

HOME AWAY FROM HOME. GLENDIVE, MONTANA.

BEER JUG BAR. GLENDIVE, MONTANA.

MOTEL ROOM. GLASGOW, MONTANA.

DIESEL SERVICING FACILITY. GLENDIVE, MONTANA.

RAILROAD CROSSING. HODGES, MONTANA.

RED SUNSET. SELDON, KANSAS.

RAILROAD DEPOT. ASH FORK, ARIZONA.

AMTRAK COAST STARLIGHT. GAVIOTA, CALIFORNIA.

WORKING UPGRADE. HODGES, MONTANA.

CONTAINER TRAIN CROSSING DRY LAKEBED. AMBOY, CALIFORNIA.

SUMMER. SIBERIA, CALIFORNIA.

ABANDONED DEPOT. CURRIE, NEVADA.

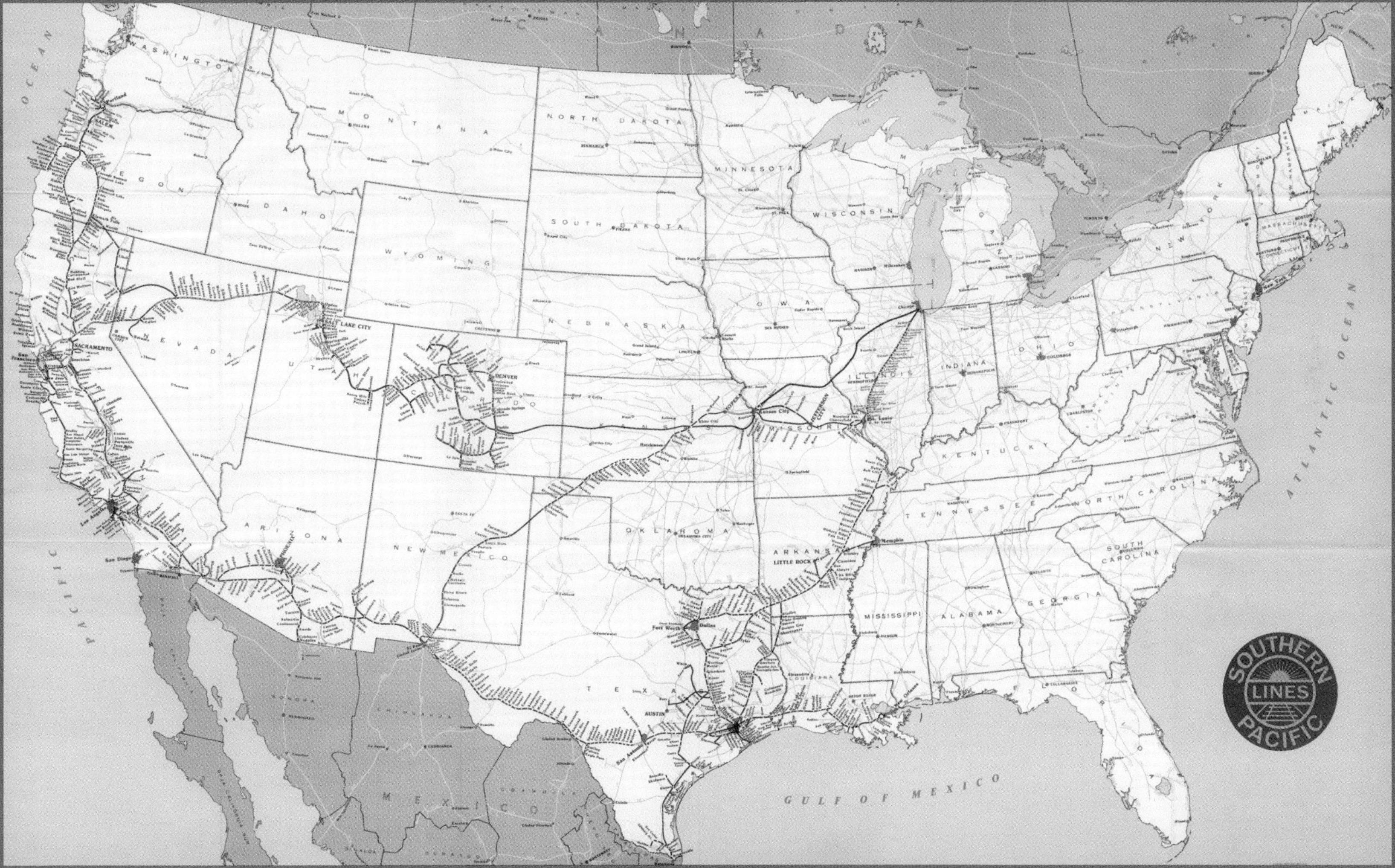
WASHINGTON
MONTANA
NORTH DAKOTA
MINNESOTA
IDAHO
WYOMING
SOUTH DAKOTA
WISCONSIN
NEBRASKA
IOWA
NEVADA
UTAH
ILLINOIS
INDIANA
OHIO
NEW YORK
KENTUCKY
TENNESSEE
NORTH CAROLINA
SOUTH CAROLINA
ARIZONA
NEW MEXICO
OKLAHOMA
ARKANSAS
MISSISSIPPI
ALABAMA
GEORGIA
TEXAS
MEXICO
SACRAMENTO
LAKE CITY
DENVER
LITTLE ROCK
AUSTIN
PACIFIC
OCEAN
ATLANTIC OCEAN
GULF OF MEXICO
SOUTHERN
LINES
PACIFIC

DESERT SUNSET. NEEDLES, CALIFORNIA.

A starry night, no coastal fog, called for the Mission Bay, on duty under the bayshore road, I have a letter from Danute, one of the free Canadians, disciple of the goddess Kali, who sleeps with men to enlighten them. La Llorona, vampire at the crossroads, she calls me her little pumpkin flower. I read the words by the overhead in my truck, zip up my Carhartt coat, step into the Mexican night, Lake Chapala in the moonlight, Danute walking a brace of Shitzus and swearing like a stevedore as they wrap her legs with their leashes. Her eyes don't match, it makes her vulnerable, that's the lure. The sucker punch follows.

"I like to wait until they think it's all going their way," she said, "and then I destroy them."

Their retaliation was also sweet. She won either way.

"I lay on a park bench in Antigua," she said. "He would decide who could have me and who could not."

I went into the shanty and met the crew, the old head foreman just nods, hands me the list.

"Get the engine out of the house and get a hold of track 3. Send them to me and line the crossovers for the main. I'm getting permission now."

I step over steel rails, counting away from the shack, the hoghead already aboard, checking the power. I put him on the cars, send him back to the old man, who will hang FRED on the rear. I kissed Danute one time, a year ago, before the ordeal.

"Why do you imagine I would sleep with you, a woman like me?"

"Some women who like sex, like sex with women, too."

Counting, I step across the rails, open the locks, pry the levers down with my foot. I have us lined across number 2 and tailing into number 1 on the main. Danute pulls away, her hand traces my scar. She is not intrigued, but now the letter.

"Back 'em up," I say, and thirty hoppers of cement fly past me in the night.

"That'll do," the conductor's growl. He's walking up. Not a good sign.

"You leave your brains at home?" he says. "You lined us into storage. Go see if we're still on the rails."

Not into one track after all. But still on the rails. Put the goddess into her box. Be here now.

HOTSHOT. LUDLOW, CALIFORNIA.

I had read many stories about journeys to the underworld. Aeneas, Dante, the hero twins in the *Popul Vuh,* Amos Tutuola in the *Bush of Ghosts,* Carlos Castaneda with his guide Don Juan—all journey to the spirit world to return enlightened and changed. The ability to do so was a basic shamanic job description. Authors claimed this ability also.

In October of 1994, my train to the underworld was ready to depart. Breast cancer was my ticket to ride. I looked at the green cottonwood tree outside the window and fixed its image as a beacon. It would go through winter and be reborn. Now the regression of being in Donna's little room made hospital sense as I agreed to six months of chemotherapy combined with three months of radiation. In more elemental terms, a sundance of poison and fire. The surgery was a piece of cake, and since I was so strong from switching freight cars and cancer is unnoticeable until it kills you, my decision to undergo treatment was an act of submission. Because I needed my arm strength to do my job, I wouldn't let them take out my lymph nodes. It was odd, to be in a poker game for body parts.

"Well, what's the point of taking them out?"

"It's diagnostic, to determine treatment."

"Well, what's the most aggressive treatment?"

"Combined chemotherapy and radiation for six months."

"Well, let's do that. So now you don't have to take out my lymph nodes."

"I guess we don't."

Tired of waiting for appointments and results, I flew to Tucson to visit Leslie, and on my way to the airport some crazed driver cut me off on the hill.

"You bastard," I yelled. "You can't kill me now; I have cancer!"

I needed to get off the grid to somewhere peaceful, a middle earth. Leslie's place was like that. Being a writer, she lived in a dreamtime among rattlesnakes and saguaros.

While I was there, she got a fax from the Zapatistas, inviting her to their second democratic convention in San Cristobal de las Casas. They had read her book *Almanac of the Dead.* She invited me to fly down with her. I agreed to go after the surgery.

And so, still taped up, I met Leslie in the Mexico City airport for the Chiapas leg. A Mexico City lefty was there to chaperone us. We stopped at a gas station in Tuxtla and bought a case of bottled water. Leslie had brought her own food. It was night when we arrived at a big town meeting with a panel of Mexico City intellectuals and a few masked Zapatistas. A big march was organized for the following day, twenty thousand indigenous people from all over Chiapas. Then we could go to the jungle to meet Marcos, they told us.

"They can see we're anarchists," Leslie said. "They won't come get us."

The next day the zocalo was filled with marchers, wearing ski masks and their indigenous dress, marking the villages they came from. I felt swept away from my own troubles and into the energy of the collective will. One might fall by the wayside, but others would move on. There were energies loose in the world, some destructive, some healing. I promised myself I would tap into the positive ones. Once again, Mexico was showing me the way.

Hanging on to my personality through the ordeal seemed futile to me. I had to let go, transform, and re-emerge afterward. As Dr. Alexander, my super-smart, no-nonsense Stanford oncologist, put the needle in my vein, I quoted Dante: "Midway through the journey of this life, I entered a dark wood."

"Pardon?" he said.

"I'm going to hell, and you're my Virgil," I said. Then I fell in love with him.

It made perfect sense. I looked forward to my chemotherapy visits and the erotic life force was with me. Life against death. Did I mention that I had a phobia about needles? Dr. Alexander shot his chemical cocktail into the back of my hand once every two weeks, while I closed my eyes and surrendered. Then I had to take more chemo pills and wait for the bottom to drop out of my metabolism and slowly climb back up, for the next round of shots and chemo pills. I would sit in his waiting room and watch the elderly patients, most of them women, come in for their weekly ordeal. I was young and strong. How did he manage to put a needle in their veins and take them to the edge of life? They were teetering on the ledge already. Unlike most doctors, Alexander empathized. He must really have believed in his treatment to risk caring the way he did.

It was now December, and I was waking every night in a pool of sweat. The chemo drop-kicked me into menopause.

"This is only temporary," I told Alexander. "I'll get my periods back."

His look said, "Maybe, but I don't think so."

I had to sleep totally naked and I would kick the covers off the bed every night. I was wearing my flimsiest shirts and couldn't tolerate anything tight around my neck. I pretended I was in the tropics,

in spite of the fact that outside the cottonwood was now yellow and shedding its leaves. My hair was also taking a hit, thinning out. The no eyelashes look. Inside a Levi Straussian duality of naked and clothed, I was among the naked. Food was a joke. I would cook dinner and throw it in the garbage. The only thing I could eat was cashew nuts and Gatorade.

The surrender to the drugs took me into an eroticized hospital world. I think this was from the absolute reversal of my normal combative mode. This was not a boxcar I could leap on and tie down. I was the one tied down, from the inside out. To be in the female world of breast cancer was a masochistic experience of the first order. To say I felt like the passive partner was an understatement. The day I got marked up with blue ink for the radiation gun I went to the most exclusive spa in Santa Cruz to recover. Alone in the Jacuzzi room my breasts were outlined with blue bull's eyes and quadrangle markings. I was beef. And could I hold still, please, absolutely still for twenty minutes while they got the gun aimed right? Again, I thought, if I can't hold my arm out like this without excruciating pain, how is some little old lady supposed to do it? Why don't they have slings or something to help you? The old industrial design question, in another guise. *Hijos de la chingada!* Not to mention that the hospital gowns in the radiologist's office were flimsy teeny-sized floral numbers that made you feel totally naked, like floozies waiting in some cathouse foyer. Can't he at least get Japanese cotton robes, with some dignified presence? I started bringing my own. I noticed it caused a ripple.

At home at Donna's, I tried to take control back through interior decoration. My bathroom, where I took the chemo pills, looked like a roadside altar to the Virgin of Guadalupe. My friends in New Mexico sent me sacred earth from Chimayo and made the pilgrimage from Santa Fe on my behalf. I asked the Church of the White Rose to add me to their prayers. When I told Leslie this, she mentioned that the sand painting that healers create around their patient is the same idea. I was creating protection around myself, creating sacred healing space. All the Mexican artifacts that I had brought back came into play now. In Mexico they were used in this way, even if the specifics had been forgotten.

Weakening from the drugs, I had started to have vivid dreams, full of animals and space travel. After one such dream, I sewed a bear suit out of fake fur, added the bear's head hat I just happened to have around from a joke I played on the engineer on the helper job in San Luis Obispo, where we took engines and pushed trains over the hill. They would put us on and off duty whenever a train showed up, so that you were goofy from the three hours sleep broken by excitement around the clock. I found the bear hat in a ski shop and ambushed the hoghead as he walked back to inspect the engines. Nearly scared him off into space. As Leslie told me, I made it just as it had appeared in my dream and hung it on the door to my room. The shaman's suit.

Other animals appeared in dreams, mostly from my Mesoamerican mythic reading over the past few years. Jaguars and fish, hero twins from the *Popul Vuh*. It wasn't the worst time of my life, by a long shot. I was willingly taking my body down to the point where it could not survive on its own, without medical support. My mind was along for the ride.

I hadn't completely abandoned my railroad personality, however. In one of the support groups I joined, the group leader wanted everyone to start a new life. On the premise that whatever I had been doing had caused the cancer, she asked me what I wanted to change.

"I've already changed everything I'm going to change," I told her. "Fuck cancer."

"What did you just say?"

"Fuck cancer," I said.

We both agreed this group just wasn't for me.

The radiation was the hardest point for me physically. Maybe it was growing up hiding under my desk during bomb drills. Now I was supposed to invite it? My body was going to have some suppressed anger over lying down for this. It was used to poison of one kind or another. But death rays? Sure enough, I got burned the first

week and stayed burned for six more. Everybody's favorite folk remedy of aloe vera caused a caustic reaction that had me in tears. I had to wear silk shirts with the labels cut out. In February I needed a blood transfusion to fight the anemia, and in March I needed daily shots to boost my white blood count. This went on for three months. My sensitive insurance company wanted me to give myself the shots. Going to an actual doctor for this seemed wasteful.

"How about I give myself radiation, too?" I asked them. "You know, jump off the table, aim the gun, set a delayed release on the trigger, and hop back on. Shouldn't be hard."

"We do care about your health," they said.

"OK, fine," I said. I kept getting the shots.

I took to sleeping on an air mattress on Donna's back lawn during the day, alternated with the couch at night. My cat, Boomer, correctly read the situation and slept on top of me the whole time. Friends who came to visit had to lie down, too, as if we were floating in a pool on lily pads. I wrote pieces of *Railroad Voices,* my second book, joking that sickness was a working person's sabbatical. Actually, that was close to the truth. The shaman's journey allowed me access to the mystical parts of my mind that normal life shuts off. Writing brought focus to these flights of imagination. It was like having my own private jet. Donna had a little plot of dirt behind her condo and I cleared it and planted a cornfield. I made blue Mayan crosses and burned copal. Everything seemed symbolic, the result of magical thinking.

I developed an obsession with gold and with having a home. I thought it was a shame to die without them.

"Even a rat has his hole," Leslie said.

I remembered another time of my life, when I was getting sober in Carrizozo, New Mexico, working on the railroad out of El Paso. In the company motel rooms, I found Gideon's Bible and in my insomnia, came upon the psalm that talks about how God is more to be desired than much fine gold, sweeter than honey in the honeycomb. It was the winds of change I embraced then, surrender to sobriety.

Now it was shelter I needed, a home, the gold hidden deep in the earth, something roots reached after. The railroad's ever-changing demands had kept me an extra board boomer my whole career. This last denial, in deference to the railroad's needs, had almost cost me my life. Now, perched in a borrowed nest, I knew how precarious my life was. For the first time, I did not feel invincible. I was a shot away from system failure. Although I did not put the conviction into action right away, the end of cancer treatment was the true end to my booming days, which were my railroad days. The freedom of the road was over for me, I just didn't know it yet.

When I came to the end of my treatment in May, I was at another crossroads. How did I get back? The roller coaster ride of chemo and recovery had stopped, but I was still weak, vulnerable, unable to eat normally, and anemic. One night I dreamed I was in an airport and had lost my bags. Nothing subtle about the unconscious. OK, trip over. Adjust. My last visit with the sexy oncologist was coming up. I had a last request, and I packed the shaman bear suit in a paper bag.

"Would you mind slipping this on for a photo op?" I said, handing him the bag. I guess nothing surprised him now.

"OK," he said, and disappeared around the corner. When he came back, half the office was with him, and he was holding a Bears mug. I sent him a copy, which he framed, and I put mine in my Virgin of Guadalupe bathroom. In the weeks that followed, I actually regretted not seeing him every day.

The cottonwood outside Donna's back door was leafing up again. What was going to be my plan for getting back to work, to life? Able to work the Colton hump last August, I now lacked the stamina to make my bed. I couldn't remember information for five minutes.

"Meet you at Shopper's Corner," someone would say, and I would promptly head off in the opposite direction, blissfully unaware. The insurance company was already calling me every week, nudging. I could resist them, but my doc Arnie told me that going back to work was an indicator of success in beating the disease. I looked around me. Santa Cruz was full of people on various kinds of disability and I didn't want to join them. It wasn't my lifestyle. But nobody, certainly no doctor I had ever encountered, understood what working on the railroad entailed. I decided to take at least four months off to get back in shape.

How far I had to go was illustrated by the fact that on two occasions, when I was going through the worst of the treatment, I had pointed a gun at my two best friends. I only remembered one of these. Donna had come home early from a trip and at two in the morning I heard a sound in the house.

"Hold it right there, motherfucker," I yelled down the hall, leveling my revolver at the shape. Luckily it was dark and Donna didn't see the gun, so she just let out her trademark glass-shattering scream. How crazy did I have to be to not remember doing the same thing when my friend Margo was staying there? What scary railroad place was I visiting in my dreams?

I hit the gym every day. In a month I had some strength, but nothing like what I used to have. The right side of my chest felt strangely frozen. I could either stay in Santa Cruz and keep pumping iron, or I could go where the culture itself was healing to me and where I felt at home. My old friend Barbara came with me and we got on a plane for Oaxaca, where we stayed with the family I had lived with while learning Spanish. I stayed there a month, a lot of it down with infections I still couldn't fight off very well. One morning I was walking down our street, when I noticed a truck pull up to the building across the street, which was a nursing home. I had walked past it many times, seeing rags drying in the open windows and medical equipment in the rooms. Two men got out of the truck and climbed the stairs. Still watching, I saw them come down with a naked man between them, one of them holding his legs, the other his arms. They walked to the back of the truck and swung the body up into the truck bed, his balls swinging in the wind. Then they got in the truck and drove away.

Mexico has a surreal way of bringing life and death together as halves of a single shell.

The message that I needed a home hit me again. Look at the human body, how fragile it is, how unexpectedly it can be claimed by the messenger dogs of the underworld, these two workers on their way to lunch. I was that naked man, and now I was alive and walking down the road.

Oaxacan colors flooded my eyes with fuchsia flowers against a deep blue wall. I felt the sun's radiation bathing my body with light. I crossed the street to walk in the shadow of the adobe walls. I was here now. I knew I was going to stay alive and bloom again.

CLIMBING ABOARD. PORTOLA, CALIFORNIA.

While I was in Mexico, writer Carol Karasik told me about a shaman named John in Santa Fe who was helping a friend of hers who had cancer. While I probably wouldn't have listened to this tip in the States, being in Mexico made me more receptive to folk wisdom. I think it was the weight that old collective beliefs had there. And so, before I returned to work, I went to Santa Fe and looked up John. He had a normal job and didn't take money for helping people. Since he worked for Blue Sky soft drinks, his office had their aluminum cans on his bookcases. I remember thinking they had very trippy can designs. He asked me to lie on a massage table and moved his hands about three inches above my body. I drifted off into a dream state and saw a beaded staff floating in the clouds. It was like I was flying above the earth.

"I don't perceive any cancer," he said. "But you need to drink lots of water. What did you see in your dream?"

I told him about the staff.

"It's life," he said. "You can return to life now."

I remembered when I first hired on in Watsonville in 1979, what a shock those first few night jobs were. I was as scared now as I had been then. The scariest thing was how easy it was for me to drift into dreamtime. This was not a good attribute on the railroad. If anything, you had to be hyper-aware. You had to make constant evaluative decisions—should I protect the point on that move or is it more important to watch the high-wide load in the middle of the

rail? Do I know how much room I have in that industry spot? Exactly how many fifty footers can go in there without going through the bumper? How are the tracks laid out? Are there potential wrong switches in any given movement? Issues like that.

And I still had to face marking up to the region/system board. Nobody from the railroad had called me to ask if I was coming back or if I needed any special assistance. It seemed like the usual sink-or-swim situation. I knew I needed to ease back in, but how? Sixteen years of experience told me that if I admitted I needed help, they would try to fire me. The railroad set up an appointment for me with their doctor, in old-time railroad lingo called a "croaker." Since the company sent him, you didn't look on him as on your side.

"Are you coming back with any restrictions?" he asked me.

I showed him the letter from my doc Arnie, stating that I was completely recovered. Not that Arnie knew what working full-time on the railroad entailed.

"OK then," he said, after a very perfunctory physical exam, "you are good to mark up."

Luckily, I could hang out on the Watsonville extra board until the region system board bids came up for October. I caught a dead-head right away to Guadalupe for two days and then a work train. All these jobs were daylight, so I could fall into the sleep of the dead after I got off. I won the RS board assignment to Oakland my first month, and John Payne was there too, staying in a motel on Jack London

Square. We caught a few jobs together, and I was aware that he was looking out for me. He took the physically harder spot working the field, leaving me the pin puller's job. On our time off we wandered around the square, ate in the cafés. Of all my railroad friends, John was the only one who had called me when I was sick. Having him around now calmed me down about being back. I knew some of the Oakland people from years of working in the Bay Area. It wasn't like walking into a hostile room each time I took a call. Still, I could tell I was not 100 percent there. I had to focus on everything I was doing, and after a few hours I got too tired. It was like my brain didn't have the oxygen to function. It took every opportunity to space out and rest. Luckily, the Oakland reserve board was not flipping every eight hours. Winter was our slow time. I made it through the month, and I had vacation time the next month, so that gave me until December to recover more.

Of course I went to Mexico, where everybody expected you to sleep in the afternoon. In December, I was in Oakland again, but the weather had turned nasty and I started catching all-nighters. Well, who could blame someone for laying off in the rain? One night I got called to flag trains through a slow order construction zone under the freeway that leads to the Bay Bridge. This freeway had collapsed in the 1987 earthquake and it was finally being repaired now. I was unfamiliar with the tracks, all they gave me was a milepost location to go to, and I was supposed to spend the night sitting in a truck with a radio to flag trains through. About 3 in the morning a local switcher went breezing past me without asking for permission. Since this was a fireable offence, I didn't know what to do. I decided to protect my job and call them on the radio, giving them "permission to pass the limits." Since I had used the radio, however, the yardmaster wanted a report and the crew then claimed I was in the wrong location, and I was aware that with no sleep I couldn't figure much of anything out. Nothing happened to the crew or me and eventually I could return to my rest at the hotel.

A week later, I caught another all-nighter at a local yard I had never been to before. The conductor was in a hurry, I was working pins, and at some point the engine split a switch and landed in the dirt. We had been sending the engine back and forth to pick up cars, but the track layout was confusing, and the night was darkness personified. Maybe I didn't line a switch. Who knows? So after the job, we had a conference with the trainmaster and nothing much was sorted out. Except that I didn't get to bed until 10 A.M. Now I had been used to these hours for fifteen years on the job. It usually took me about two weeks to get used to the crazy sleep patterns, but now things were different. Now the hours were really messing me up.

In January, I had some minor surgery to take a foreign object out of my thumb. Two days afterward, with stitches, I left to work in LA.

"Are you sure I can work with this thumb?" I asked the surgeon. "You know I work on the railroad." Years of trying to explain my work to doctors had made me cynical.

"Shouldn't be any problem," he said.

A week later I had an infected thumb. With the rain, the railroad greasy dirt, and having to take gloves on and off, I just couldn't keep it clean, not to mention that I actually used my thumb to hang on to the sides of railroad cars. A company "croaker" gave me a week off to heal and then told me to mark back up. I still had a huge bandage on my hand and I couldn't really get a good grip with it. This doctor was a German immigrant and I could tell he thought I was trying to cheat the company by getting days off or something. Since days off were unpaid, I really couldn't sympathize with his point of view.

I marked back up to a rainy night and caught the Long Beach "oil can" job. It was an all-night job that switched out the petroleum plants near the port. "Oil cans" were the tank cars that we handled all night. My foreman hated boomer brakemen and was a cowboy of the first order.

"I been on this job three months and lost 10 pounds. Really gets you in shape. Just try to keep up," he said, ignoring the bandaged thumb I was trying to stuff into my waterproof gloves. He then set his normal pace, which was a dead run, and sent me to ride the point on cars to industries I'd never been to before, giving last-minute instructions to catch a tanker on the fly or to suddenly bail off. At a certain point, hanging on to the awkward handhold on a tank, getting ready to bail off, I met a part of me I had never met before, and I instantly trusted it.

"Hey, you," it said, "we're not doing this anymore."

"Can we discuss this at another moment?" I said.

"No," it said. "We're not doing this anymore."

"All right," I said. "You win. I'm going in the yard."

My body was right. All the strange things that had been happening to me at work in the past three months were adding up. I had always said that I would quit if I couldn't do the job, and now I had to look at what I could do. The company was trying to force surplus brakemen into the so-called "shortage" yards, where they would be unable to exercise their seniority to leave. Switchmen made a lot less money than brakemen, unless they worked eight-on and eight-off around the clock. My local yard did not have a midnight shift, so that option was not available. The lack of a midnight shift, however, made it my only choice to get the rest necessary to recover. I was looking at a one-third pay cut. But I knew I had to do it. I just didn't have the stamina to be out working all night in new territory where you had to be hyper-vigilant since you didn't know where the switches were or what the tracks looked like. Another factor pressuring me was that this year would be the basis for any wage settlement after the Union Pacific took over. What I made this year would determine any guarantee under the New York Dock Agreement. If I made a low salary, I would never have a safety net in my subsequent railroad career.

I was familiar with the concept of surrender from the twelve-step program I had been working for thirteen years. But it was still hard. I didn't mind turning things over to a higher power, but I didn't want that power to be the Southern Pacific Railroad.

Later that night, during our twenty-minute beans, one of the other region/system boomers gave me a suspicious stare.

"You that gal who wrote that lyin' book?"

"Which specific so-called lie are you referring to?" I asked

"Well, I ain't read it, I just heard about it."

"Well, in other places in the world, besides Utah, I mean, people actually read books before they talk about them."

It was mean of me. As Alex, the night clerk at the Resetar Hotel in Watsonville, used to say, "I refuse to engage in a battle of wits with an unarmed person."

While I was in LA, probably just to make sure I didn't change my mind, I had another reminder that I needed to come home. I was down at the oil can yard again, but in daylight and with a decent crew. All the switches in the yard were variable, meaning that you could run through them with equipment and the wheels would flip the switch over to the new direction. If the company did not maintain them or if some debris got caught in the points, they could have enough of a gap to derail a car on a facing point movement. The company was always issuing bulletins for various places instructing us to treat all switches as rigid, even if they were variable. The hoghead on our crew told me they just ran through them anyway here. When you were working in a new place, you had to find out which rules were followed and which ones were ignored. On one of our moves, we shoved through a variable switch with the engine and picked up a line of piggyback flatcars on another lead. Our next move was then to shove these cars back the direction we had come, over that switch, now lined for our movement. As I went to get on the leading car to ride the point, I couldn't find a comfortable handhold, since the cargo was too close to the weird ladder these cars were equipped with. These new ladders actually angled away from the cars, forcing any rider to lean backward while holding on with upper body strength alone. It was a pet peeve of mine that new industrial design never considered the human who had to utilize it. New cars were harder to ride, harder to get on and off of, harder to tie brakes on, not easier. What was the design for, then?

And so I let the first car go by, and boarded the second car. As the first car passed over the switch, the wheels caught the points and the entire car flipped over before my eyes. Well, clearly that variable switch wasn't working too well, and technically I should have been on the point to check it, but you know, I was so glad I wasn't because I doubt I would have seen it and it would have been me under the wheels. In our meeting with the trainmaster, we filled out an accident report and that was the end of it. But even if the trainmaster wasn't particularly upset by the car ending up in the dirt, I was aware that this was my second derailment in two months. After my rookie years, derailments just didn't happen to me. I had never been to an investigation in my whole railroad career. I had never used my job protection insurance. Company officers never knew my name, a condition the trainmaster who hired me said was optimum. Now I needed a haven, no matter how much it cost me in pay. In March I transferred to the San Jose yard as a switchman, knowing that for the first time in my railroad history, I was stuck somewhere. It felt like I was making a last stand.

DEPOT PARKING LOT. TUCUMCARI, NEW MEXICO.

I thought of San Jose as the hospital yard because everyone seemed to have something grave the matter with them, as I did. We were all cripples or those rare saints who preferred time with their families to a big paycheck. My foreman that day was Jessie Cervantes, who was 64 years old and limped. When he saw me he looked disappointed because he figured he would have to do a lot more work than he wanted to. A switchman named Squeaky was here because he was called back off disability after fifteen years driving a school bus; Charlie was a throat cancer survivor who worked like a horse but could hardly talk on the radio. Before you worked with him often enough to anticipate what he wanted before he said it, there were these tragicomic moments when you would be hanging off a boxcar getting directions on the move.

"Dwopfreeovethswimeemeeiorale."

"What was that, Charlie?"

"DWOPFREEOVETHSWIMEEMEEIORALE."

And of course you didn't want to ask him a third time over the radio because everyone was listening from San Francisco to Hollister and you wouldn't understand it any better anyway.

Judd, the 74-year-old engineer, ex-bartender, quick-draw artist, and man with a thousand jokes, was here because his gambling habit had made a mess of his retirement plans. Gary, a big guy on his second heart attack, who, eighteen years ago when I hired out, had the job of keeping me from killing myself the first night, was fond of

saying things like, "Now Linda, if I keel over out there, you're gonna have to carry me." It was a real possibility. He would never take a break and insisted on riding on the rear knuckle of our cut of cars miles back to the yard. Dave, who had three years until retirement, was known as "the laziest man on the railroad." The number-one man on the seniority list had drinking problems that caused him to lay off a third of the year. Our road foreman of engines was a little like Richard Nixon in his later days. Any question you asked him entered a Möbius strip of dialogue that took hours and resulted in bitter misunderstandings. I tried to raise a safety issue once with him about the tracks the maintenance-of-way workers were using to repair cars. In San Jose, such tracks were just blue flagged in the middle of the rail, instead of locked out at the switch at each end of the track. Switchmen got a daily reprieve from sending cars over the maintenance-of-way derail only by exercising extreme caution in using the live rail. The road foreman responded by telling the maintenance-of-way foreman that I said he was working dangerously.

"I heard from Numb Nuts that you said we was operating without protection."

"Consider the source, Lou. I never said that."

"Well, it's a damn lie whoever said it."

The road foreman's big opportunity for spiritual growth occurred shortly after the Union Pacific takeover when he was ushering some UP officials around the territory on a high-railer. He dutifully got permission to occupy Amtrak's 1 Rail and then hopped out on 2 Rail and went nose-to-nose with a train. Now that is an easy mistake to make since 2 Rail is renamed 1 Rail past a certain milepost. Nobody but Amtrak would set it up that way. We were just glad that an official and not a conductor fell into the trap. Not that it changed his consciousness in any way. He came back from his punishment tour in Texas even more zealous in ferreting out our mistakes. His credibility problem was that we all knew nobody cared about our yard or us. The trainmaster's office was empty, the trainmaster having deserted our funky yard for the new Union Pacific yard at Milpitas, where presumably he didn't have mice running over his desk all day. His personality was wallpaper anyway, and he would only show up under duress if some accident occurred for which he had to order a pee test. He would drive through the yard once a month on his way to Milpitas, and that was it.

We did have our blessings, however. Bob Blinkenberg, the afternoon yardmaster, was the sun that shone on the San Jose yard. He'd been a Southern Pacific officer briefly, and he was the only one the trainmen never complained about. When it got too hectic, he went back yardmastering. He always chose to protect his family life, living in a house trailer by the golf course and never wanting his wife to work. As a brakeman on the road, whenever you came through Blink's yard, he always had a greeting and a compliment on the radio for you. It was like letters from home. His system in the yard was to get everybody out of one another's hair. If he gave you permission to come into the yard, he always had you lined up for your move so that everything went smoothly. Working for Blink, you hardly ever saw another crew, much less collided with them. He gave early quits—which was an endearing trait—but crews worked hard for them. If you finished your lists, you went home, and generally the yard crews had their work done and were out of the way by nightfall, the time the locals and through freights started needing the yard to pick up and set out cars. If there was an emergency after the crews

went home, Blink would handle it himself. During the afternoon, you always saw him lacing air hoses, and, if necessary, moving bad-ordered cars along with an iron bar and his Chevy Suburban carryall. That carryall held hickory blocks, wrenches, pry bars, pipes, knuckles, and spare air hoses. My first night in the yard with Jessie, Blink showed up with his truck when the several reefers we kicked down 10 Rail ended up in the dirt.

It had been raining steadily for weeks. The old rotten ties that most of the rails were resting on were now sunken in various spots, and cars hitting other stopped cars in the rails were likely to turn over in these soft spots, or the rails themselves would spread from the impact. Blink pulled the Chevy up next to the derailed car and Jessie and I tried to give him a hand stacking the hickory blocks in a ramp leading to the top of the rail from the inside of the derailed wheel. We would use the engine to couple to the derailed car and gradually inch it up the blocks, hopefully back onto the rail.

"Not much help here, are we?" Jessie kidded him. "An old man and a girl."

"I think that'll do it," Blink said, and he gave the engineer an "ease 'em back slowly" sign, watching the wheels strain to climb the hickory blocks and drop into place between the outside rails.

"That'll do right there," he signed the engineer. And we were back in business until we got a hold of 8 Rail and started pulling it out through the main crossovers and went on the ground all over again.

"That's it for the night, boys," Blink told us, shaking his head. "This is one for the hook."

The whole yard was ready to fall apart at any time. That's what made knowing it so difficult. You had to know all its quirky spots and its work-around-it compromises that everybody there knew but the newcomer would stumble into doing the easiest moves. It was part of breaking in. Like getting a name, or setting the tone for getting along with everybody.

"When I first got here," Jessie told me, "I told people 'Hey, I'm a Latin lover. That means I'm a fucking Mexican.' Because I said it, they had to laugh with me. And they let me in."

I had already achieved a partial détente in the yard by virtue of having hired out in Watsonville, thirty miles away. If I hadn't worked with everybody before, they had at least heard about me, if not that I was an OK worker then at least that I had written a book about railroading and hence had some kind of juice somewhere. I had already told all the dirt there was to tell on myself, and here I still was out working. My current problem, however, was the problem that landed me in the San Jose yard in the first place—I still wasn't back to normal from cancer treatment. As a new switchman in the yard, and, of course, as a new woman switchman in the yard, I had to do the usual proving of myself all over again. But now I was handicapped. I couldn't work as hard as I used to and I occasionally needed help. Working for Blink was a godsend because he made it so easy to do my job, and if I messed up, he quickly forgave me and I could show up tomorrow and it would be a new day.

Of course, being on the extra board I got stuck working with everybody's least favorite foreman, Dave, who had a permanent helper vacancy on his job. It was vacant because on Dave's job the helper did all the work. Dave held the notion that foremen or conductors just tell other people to work—an idea outmoded by the fact that there were now only two people on a crew at most and often only one. When I worked with Dave, the day became a long chess game to see if I could maneuver him into throwing one more switch or lacing one more hose than he had already calculated into his routine.

"Have you yelled at him yet?" fellow switchmen would ask me.

I thought of him as "Dave at the switch," because that's where he would be during most of the moves, including one wet afternoon when he sent me riding the point into an industry track submerged over the wheels of the boxcars. After a while, I started calling him to come back and help me take off brakes or throw hard switches, but Dave would then try to subtract for that extra effort some other move he would usually make. It was like trying to reprogram a mule. It just wasn't going to happen. Charlie, the hardest working man on the railroad, would actually lay off when called to work on Dave's crew. Paradoxically, though, working for Dave, and with the assistance of Blink's early quits, I started to get my strength back and to feel my physical body once more molded by the work.

As with most peaceful reprieves, this one was destined to disappear. Two events were happening to us that would change our working lives. The Union Pacific was taking over our railroad and Bob Blinkenberg was leaving us.

Blink's retirement dinner was the scene of much heartfelt grief and, in fact, actual tears. The switchmen had assembled all the implements of his office and presented him with these items spray-painted gold. We all knew that light was about to be replaced by outer dark. His replacement on the afternoon shift, a yardmaster known as the Buddha, was about to start running the yard. Before he left us, Blink had said this to me: "You know, I've managed to get through the whole afternoon without yelling at anyone or belittling anyone or humiliating anyone. I feel sorry for you guys."

The Buddha was named in the spirit of oxymoron. He weighed around 300 pounds and he smelled like the underside of something. Blink, taking over from Buddha's morning shift, used to spray his chair, desk, and phone with something called "Kill." The Buddha's physical problems kept him restricted to yardmastering and rumors of problems in other yards hung around him like dark clouds.

"I'm not Blink," he said. "And things are going to be different around here. The way I see it, my job is to be an asshole."

The yard after dark changed from a scene of ships passing in the night to a three-ring circus, with Buddha as the ringmaster. As a matter of fact, he had even tried to get a job as trainmaster on the circus train. He loved to be in the middle of a mess, giving orders. He thrived on opposition.

The dark side to the Buddha's character was a surprise to me, since I had only known him when I was a brakeman bringing a train from Watsonville into the yard. He would show up at the caboose and take the crew on a wild ride to the other end of the yard where our new cut of cars was waiting for the return trip. Apart from the absurd speed flying down the tracks in the dark (which I liked, anyway), he was cordial and even somewhat charming. To work for him in the yard, however, was another story. In the yard, he wanted total control. And he turned out to be rabidly anti-woman.

The Buddha announced his new agenda by telling all the crews they had to stay the full eight hours, even if all they did was sit around. If you came in early, he would find things for you to do, like going to pull out a track and put it somewhere else. Then, if you caught the next morning's job, you would have to put it back where it was before. This kind of thing was not only irritating, it was stupid. Any move on the railroad could be the scene of an accident. An unnecessary move was merely some new opportunity for someone to get hurt. Everyone seemed to have the same bright idea—that if I were to get the Buddha fired for harassment, we would have our sweet little jobs back. This idea was based on the prejudice and fantasy that all any woman had to do was cry "sexual harassment" and, justly or unjustly, heads would roll. This was the exact opposite of the truth. Railroad management couldn't even spell "harassment." Knowing this, I had scrupulously settled my own problems on the railroad for the last eighteen years, but prejudice being what it is, every day was a new day with the same old ideas floating untouchably in the blue sky. And so they goaded me with every idiot thing the Buddha would say about me behind my back.

"You know you're on his list, don't you?" Charlie said. "According to Russ, everything wrong about this whole operation is your fault."

The source of the Buddha's tenacity was that the San Jose yard was his last stand. He was starting to virtually live at the yard, like the homeless he patrolled for in the carryall. For a while he yardmastered by day and drove commercial trucks at night, then fell back to putting in overtime for free and dropping by or listening on the radio on weekends, sleeping in the yard office, and joining a rail buff club that met in the Amtrak depot that fronted on the yard. He always took December off, giving the switchmen what they referred to as a bonus vacation, but turned up at Christmas with a tree for the yard office and the wistful side of his personality polished up a little.

After Blink left, nobody else cared for the yard. Certainly nobody ever cleaned the office again. The garbage cans filled with rotting trash. Caked mud stayed on the floors. The Buddha never cleaned himself up and certainly would never actually mop anything the way Blink used to do. It took a mass protest by the switchmen to compel the Buddha to buy three new XXXL T-shirts so that they could stand to be in the carryall with him. The carryall driver's seat, used by him daily, had no springs left and had sunk to such a level that when I had to use it once, I could not see over the steering wheel.

But the trainmasters knew that if they left him alone, Buddha would handle the yard. And so we were at sea in the hospital ship with our own Ahab, missing his leg and ordering the switchmen about as if they were the missing appendage. He regarded me with the grudge usually reserved for the whale.

Our first big fight was over the women's bathroom key, which Buddha wanted to control. Unlike the men's bathroom, the women's bathroom was hardly used, and he liked to keep it locked in order to reserve it for his personal use. This meant that before my shift I had to go through the ritual of asking him for the key, which he would withhold while he called some customer a "cocksucker" on the phone or chatted with the train dispatcher. Having my own key would allow me to short-circuit this little daily drama and so I asked him for an extra one. Soon we were in a face-off.

"You don't need that goddamn key and you're not going to get it!"

"What was that? Could you shout a little louder? Maybe there's some part of this I'll understand if you shout more."

"I'm going to goddamn well shout if I goddamn well feel like it and you don't need no goddamn key."

"Well, thank you. That's all very clear now. You've made your point very clearly. I think I've got it word for word."

In spite of the fact that I had written two books on life on the rails, the Buddha refused to contemplate that this conversation of ours might find its way into print. That was about my only leverage, in the absence of company supervision in the yard, and so I let it drop to the switchmen that I was "keeping a book" on Buddha. And, in fact, I started to. About every three months I would have to go nose-to-nose with him about something—calling me "Linda Lou" on the radio, giving instructions to my helper instead of me when I was foreman, contradicting my instructions to my crew halfway through moves in the yard, generally putting out the message that it was OK to disrespect me. While I was working in the yard, it always seemed not worth it to stop everything and make a scene with Buddha, but if I let it go, he would escalate. So every couple of months, I would have to stop the action on the lead and walk into the yard office and confront him.

"Why aren't you out working? I know you're not done yet!"

"My name is Linda, not Linda Lou. Linda Lou is a pet name and I am not your pet. When I hear 'Linda Lou' I get confused and I have to stop everything and come talk to you, or the trainmaster, about it. Just to make sure I know exactly who you are referring to."

"You just get back out there and do your work. I'm tired of all this stalling around."

"Just remember," I said, thinking aneurysm, "the more you yell, the slower I go."

Since the Buddha was on afternoons, the foreman spot became undesirable since the foreman had to deal directly with him. With the least seniority of anybody in the yard, I was often nominated. Work took the shape of a tug-of-war with the Buddha on one side, the crew on the other, and the foreman in the middle. Take, for example, the question of going to beans. When the crews left early,

they worked straight through beans, sometimes stopping for coffee in the districts when it was convenient and wouldn't delay them too much. Now, working the full eight hours, they wanted beans and a coffee break, too. The game had changed to pacing ourselves. The Buddha would forbid me to take a coffee break in the district, but in the district, I was the boss. The big problem was getting the crew not to throw their Big Gulp cups from Carl's on the lead in front of the yard office on the way back in. Of course, not going to coffee was never rewarded since when we got back to the yard we immediately got more work to do, until we were hard up against our union contract right to eat at four hours thirty minutes on duty. By this time we were in the middle of switching cars at the far end of the yard from the shanty. Then, when the crew wanted to eat, I had to call the Buddha on the radio and get into it with him. After a few such days, I called the trainmaster to prepare him for a showdown. He grudgingly acknowledged our right to take the same amount of time to eat as other crews.

"Come on," I said. "It's ludicrous, his trying to deprive us of food. Does he look like he's missed any meals lately?"

"He looks like he could stand to miss a few," he said.

And so, when Buddha roared up in the carryall, crunching gravel, and started yelling that "OK then, you got twenty minutes to be back here working," I told him, "We'll be back after we've had sufficient time to eat."

"Well, we'll just see what the trainmaster says about that."

"Get him on the phone. I talked to him last night."

His face went purple, but he didn't spontaneously combust. Instead, he roared back down the lead, leaving us to make our way to lunch on foot. The engineer, who had been watching all this from the cab, said, "There goes our five-minute quit."

In about the middle of August in that first year of our captivity, I caught Dave's afternoon job, which now felt like a haven since, as foreman, he had to deal with the yardmaster. It so happened that the Buddha hated him even more than he did me. They had an old antagonism and in all that time Buddha had never been able to get the better of him. Dave was just too slick. After answering the usual bellow summoning him into the office, Dave emerged with handfuls of the Buddha's tortured switch lists, page after page marked "1, 1A, 1B," and so on, detailing in his idiosyncratic code exactly how he wanted things done. Asking for clarification made him belligerent.

"How long you been out here and you can't read a goddamn list! I know you went out there last week!"

He delighted in using old arcane track numbers, ones that only he and the old heads remembered the significance of.

"All you have to do is tell us what rail it is. It's a lot shorter than asking all these pointless rhetorical questions."

That day we had a lot to do in the yard before we gathered up our district cars and headed for the 5 Zone. A hundred cars off the San Jose hauler were sitting on 3 Rail, waiting to be bled and classified, and we had cars for the two locals to switch out too. I set out walking down 4 Rail bleeding cars, only to meet up with Buddha in the carryall as I worked my way back down 3. He was leaning out the window using a hook to pull the bleed rods.

"Get in here; I'll give you a ride. You know if Dave won't do his job, you just tell me about it and I'll make sure he does."

I guess he thought it would be such a relief to have him off my back I'd jump right on the "hate Dave" bandwagon.

"You know, don't you, that the more you and Dave fight, the more work I have to do. So I'll just deal with Dave myself, OK?"

"I know he hides out in the district. He goes to coffee at Carl's, doesn't he?"

"He's the foreman. He can go to coffee if he wants to."

"No, he can't. I say who can go to coffee."

Leaving me at the east end he rumbled off, finding roads among the rails, looking for winos, and policing his yard. Dave and I settled into our lead job dance, him kicking the cars and me throwing the switches, trying to pace myself and not have to run, watching the lists, staying one step ahead of the next cut of cars. It was almost

restful, Dave being such a creature of habit that I could count on him never to vary his moves. Slow, yes, but steady.

At about 8 PM the summer sun had gotten off our backs on the lead, and 3 Rail was cleared off and stowed away on our local's sluff tracks, and we had 6 Rail tied and pulled down to the east end and set with a brake for the Watsonville hauler, and the Broadway's cars sent up a clear rail to the west end, with the Mission Bay's pickup behind them. Our own cars were dug out and lined up on the lead, laced, air tested, and FRED hung on the last car, and now we could set about our own district work—about four hours' worth if we ran beans and just worked straight through, although now there was no percentage in doing that. In a situation like this, Dave always went for the overtime, hiding out for an hour in Burger King and another hour in Carl's, regaling me with his three subjects—the high cost of living, the necessity for regular exercise (because he didn't get much on the job), and the plot of whatever movie he had just seen. The full moon had started to rise as we received permission, in the form of a green signal, from the dispatcher to cross his main line to enter the Union Pacific's Milpitas branch. Our first industry was a paper house close by, and I was putting on my gloves to go out the door and bail off when we heard Eddie Mesa on the Watsonville hauler going through the depot at San Jose.

"Calling the San Jose yardmother, over," Eddie crooned in a Cheech-and-Chong-like violation of proper radio procedure.

"Yes, my son, you call?" the Buddha's voice not at all the hostile hot air we had met with all day, but a radio voice reaching out to sensitive ears, traversing distances and boundaries, gentle, mocking, and seductive. Our very own Tokyo Rose.

We all stopped in our tracks and listened. The big yellow moon struggled above the warehouse walls and the night crickets started their songs.

"And do you wish to enter my fair yard?" The Buddha spoke the words as if the prince was at the ball, the slipper in hand, the fix in with the pumpkin. He was, in a word, beautiful again.

"Well, what do you think of that?" Dave said.

"His yard? That fat fuck," the engineer said. "We know what a toad he is."

"My fair yard!"

The Watsonville hauler was going by the Y switch now and gave us a toot and a hello. "Hey good lookin'," Eddie came over the radio again. The first night I worked with him eighteen years ago, he left me at a hard-to-throw switch on a drop, sent the engine past me, and I had about two minutes to get the switch over so the ten loaded boxcars rolling free could get by me. Afterward he told me, "I got some advice for you on the railroad, kid. Cover your ass." He had mellowed into a pretty nice guy.

I thought about the Watsonville yard, now long gone, where I had hired out and that used to feel like home. Was I at home in San Jose? Although I could put in an eight-hour day switching now, I had nothing left for my life. I had started to eliminate love affairs and time with friends, and even walking the three blocks to the beach seemed too hard after work. And as for work itself, was San Jose my fair yard? Sometimes I'd walk the rails first thing on duty, bleeding the cars and reading the spray can graffiti and photographing it. Maybe forty minutes out of the day, it could be my yard, too. But by and large, everybody had to think about Buddha all the time. Every conversation contained the obligatory prayers: "Hope that fat fuck keels over today."

"He was sick last week. It's getting to him, the pressure."

"Maybe he won't last the year."

The Buddha was at the center of a vortex created entirely by himself. His yard was something that absolutely could not be shared. It was his magic site to work his will and boss around his switchman slaves in order to create a perfect, beautiful place, visited by passing trains, part of the long bloodstream of traffic in the night, the river he used to navigate driving trucks because he could not go home. I realized I was already planning to leave this work to find a home. But he was at home there now, like me, restricted to the yard, but unlike me—having no other love and nowhere else to go. It was more his than mine. He was the railroad. I just worked there.

RAILROADER COFFEE BREAK. GLENDIVE, MONTANA.

The industry track at Granite Rock was a little pastoral interlude on the district job. Not that the tracks and switches were in good condition, or the adjacent junkyard pull was not treacherous. The granite dust on summer days made you reach for your bandana or a dust mask for your face, if you had to be out in the fine powder the engine kicked up. The tracks leading in ran along Coyote Creek, which kept its natural shape, only occasionally sandbagged to shore up the trailer park hidden near its entrance, a residential enclave sandwiched between Georgia Pacific, a tank farm called Cap Snap and Seal, and City Metals. I always felt the presence of the invisible people in the trailer park living there beside the creek, off the grid of Silicon Valley, hidden inside its industrial maze. The railroad ran behind the façade. Other people found shelter there as well, the homeless urban campers whose cardboard homes I increasingly thought of as "California condos." Our move at Granite Rock was to pull loads and deliver empties, while watching out for the Sikh truck drivers lining up at the artificial pyramids of sand to do the same. Making a joint one day, radio in hand, sweating blindly into my dirt-coated overalls, a Sikh driver chatted me up.

"Hello. You have a good job. You want to meet a working man? I am a good person. I go to temple."

There was a certain magic to the place. While I was waiting for my braking partner to run around the cars or pull the spots, I would sometimes look into the woods by the creek bank, amazed that something natural could continue its life here. Like the wild datura blooming beside the tracks at night, the shape of the land revealed itself. The spiritual beauty of the rails pulled back the myopic lens, showing another history, another life inside what I assumed was life.

Of course, it was here that I would find the portrait of a Mexican devil on the porch of a hopper car. California has a long history of Mexican labor, starting, of course, when it was Mexico. Since those days, people have moved back and forth across the line in the sand, the railroad being the road to ride. The Santa Clara and Salinas valleys have mostly converted from agribusiness to high tech, but remnants remain, and pickers still come with the seasons here. They also work other jobs, but Silicon Valley salaries have made rentals out of reach, so they sleep on mattresses beside the rails, in the Hotel Mira Estrellas, the Hotel Look at the Stars. I would read in the paper that crash space on someone's floor was going for $200 a month, so in these hidden railroad districts, what I was seeing were working men, as well as winos, making the unpoliced railroad space their home.

As in LA, there was gang graffiti on the warehouse walls facing the tracks, and tag crews often marked the cars in the yard, leaving their empty cans in the toe paths, a true hazard for trainmen in the dark. This artist, however, had taken his time. The entire sloping rear porch of the cement hopper was covered with a black-and-white portrait of the Spanish devil of the Inquisition, a face I had seen on countless Mexican dance masks. The more I understood about

Mexico, the more I saw that we were like intertwined hands. Mexican folk art was practiced here, at Granite Rock, and in the tagged graffiti, *nalgas de oro, Cañas, Zacatecas* (butt cheeks of gold), from a little town north of Zacatecas. I made a note to try to go there sometime, the home of *nalgas,* who was here working in my home.

I thought about what the railroad had taught me about where I lived and who else was living there. I saw things that normal citizens never saw. Working LA, I found myself in Echo Park at 2 AM contemplating gang graffiti under freeway overpasses, all alone with a radio at the end of a mile-long train. I knew where migrant laborers washed in the Guadalupe River just off the 880 Freeway in San Jose. Our day job crossed the trestle each morning, and I saw their possessions hung out to dry on tumbleweeds. Traveling by bus in ever-expanding circles from Mexico City each time I had vacations, I started to recognize where in Mexico the immigrants came from by their features and dress. I now felt comfortable at immigrant stores buying Mexican matches and tamarind candy and Guadalupe candles.

In Veracruz at a crafts show I bought a devil mask from a sculptor who lived in Naulinco. He was saving it for a show, but when I dreamed about it and came back, he sold it to me. This was the face that was on the cement hopper at Granite Rock. I had hired out in Watsonville Junction, learning switching in the salad bowl districts of Salinas, while Mexicans worked picking the strawberries, lettuce, asparagus, broccoli, Brussels sprouts, and artichokes. The tracks bisected the fields, the big yellow buses and porta-potties were parked right next to the rails. The workers in hats, long sleeves, and bandanas, worn against the sun and pesticides, worked alongside our train.

Years later, I needed a taxi from Patscuaro to Morelia in Michoacán. It was a long ride and I searched the taxis parked along the street for an honest face. An older man met my gaze and we agreed on a price. On the two-hour ride, we found out we both had been working in Salinas in 1979. He saved his money, returned home to his family, and bought his taxi.

"You had a successful life," I said. I was aware that my life wasn't as settled. But then, I was still working in California.

At the bus station, he carried my bags and hugged me like a brother.

Railroad boomers make good money and see themselves as middle class, but they have much in common with migrants. Work defines our lives, work "from can till can't," as they say in Texas. We both leave home and live provisionally, in motels with grease-stained carpets on the upper end or in literal holes in the ground, for the pickers living in caves. We are all really working for other people, with our families far away, or having a deferred family life in the case of railroaders. We are not in the class that gets rich. Our bodies are our livelihood. Railroaders call themselves rails—what the railroad runs on. It was not a far leap to see the others that industry runs on as more like me than not, particularly when they were working beside me in the fields, factories, and industrial plants.

TRUCK STOP. PINE BLUFF, WYOMING.

In the twenty years that I'd worked for the railroad, I had rarely held a regular job. I was a boomer, never a home guard. This was partly circumstance and partly inclination—in the years after I hired out in 1979, Southern Pacific eliminated three out of five jobs on a crew, so I followed the work and returned home to Watsonville Junction where I could hold the extra board for beet season in the spring and fall. Being the baby on extra boards all over the Southwest gave me certain skills, such as working with different types of equipment, seeing how more experienced crews did things, seeing different operations like mines, petrochemical yards, agricultural districts, and city jobs. A boomer quickly sizes up new track layouts, bowl and hump yards, and main line track systems. But you never get really skilled at one particular job and you never develop the rhythm of working with the same people year after year. You are always the awkward person on the job, the one who slows things down and reminds the regular crew how very talented and brilliant they really are.

It wasn't until I abandoned the booming life and became a switchman in the San Jose yard that I could hold a regular job. San Jose only had four regular jobs a day, no midnight shift, and a four-man extra board. The morning jobs made up the Hollister local and the pickup for the San Jose turn. Then they switched out Granite Rock and a few industries up the Agnews branch. The afternoon jobs switched the San Jose turn's setout, made up the Mission Bay's pickup, and set the Broadway local. Then one job went to places we called 5 Zone and 3 Zone, and one job, the Lawrence switcher, went up Amtrak's commute corridor to switch the butter house and the paper house on one side of the double main line and a rock house on the opposite side.

The foreman's job on the Lawrence switcher was demanding because Amtrak officials would yell at the foreman if a commute train got a yellow signal when the switcher was late going east. The foreman was the one the crew would blame if they didn't get their early quit.

"Too much pressure on this job," the foreman who held the number one spot on the seniority list told me one day, waiting at Lawrence. "It's a nice June day; it's not raining. Why split a gut worrying about getting back to the yard?"

I admired his attitude and even shared it, but the macho crews wouldn't let a foreman take that stance. They were all out to prove they could run within that window and get back to the yard early. They expected the foreman to go with the flow. When I first came into the San Jose yard, I was rarely the foreman, since all the regular jobs were bid in and I was the baby. But all that changed when our unpopular yardmaster bid in the afternoon shift. Suddenly, you couldn't give that job away. It went to the extra board every day.

Soon, the company force-assigned the junior switchman to the foreman's spot and the junior switchman was me.

Luckily, though, I also acquired a decent regular crew when my old friend John Payne came in the yard. He was also a refugee from the twenty-day away-from-home brakeman's board, but unlike most of us, he seemingly had nothing wrong with him. As a matter of fact, John, at 51, still had a runner's body. He brought a cooler of juice and healthy snacks to work and really hated going to beans when he could trade the hour for one at the end of the day. He looked like an aged 19-year-old. And he had been my first conductor on my student trips when I had hired out eighteen years ago.

"I stood up for you," John told me, "when the other guys wanted to run you off. I told them, 'Look, she has never been in a railroad yard before. It is all new.' I told them you could do the job."

"And you were right," I said, since he was looking as if he didn't quite believe it. But that was John's chivalrous thing.

John had to bid in the helper's spot, even though he could hold the foreman's because that way he could work with me instead of a switchman known as "El Loco," who wouldn't work as a foreman. John outbid him as my helper, thereby giving us a regular job that was bearable, even though we were working for the yardmaster from hell. John had tried being foreman, but the yardmaster's constant interference got him rattled.

Sometimes John described his own father as a war hero and other times as a chief of police, but the defensive tone in his voice told me that John had been afraid of him. Standing up to authority made John nervous, but then, during the Viet Nam War, he had refused induction eight times. "I am the most inducted man in history," he used to say. Eventually, the army just left him alone. He would recount that history to me on midnight telephone monologues, after some trying day when he felt he had backed down. Our system was this: I let him run the job from the field man's position, and I dealt with the yardmaster. We split up the really onerous tasks, like riding the point on the six-mile shove out to Lawrence and back.

"John's really happy now," the engineer told me one night. "He's in love."

It was our railroad marriage. We'd talked before about getting married and doubling our railroad retirement benefits, but an undercurrent of seriousness lay beneath the joke. Neither one of us wanted to risk what we already had—a long-distance flirtation with someone who lived next door, sex talk on the phone, a safe relationship. We rarely visited each other's houses. Maybe two or three times in twenty years. But then, with John, nobody did. One time El Loco just dropped by and John heard him outside his door. John hid out until he left and then ranted about it for weeks at work.

We'd get our yard switching done in the afternoon, make up three or four locals and finish switching out the San Jose turn from Oakland. Then we would go to beans, and John would pull out his cooler from his Datsun pickup and chow down on health drinks, energy bars, raw veggies, and sandwiches. He weighed about 150 and still fit into JC Penney slim cords and white T-shirts. His boots were worn through, but a trip shopping was out of the question. John liked to shop for food, though, and lunchtime was usually spent recounting how well he fed his friend Jean and her cat, who loved to eat grilled shrimp. He had dated Jean in his Viet Nam War resister days and still went to see her every afternoon in her trailer park in Aptos. He credited her with saving his life. She was a lot older than John, and, other than myself, was his only confidant. Once John let you in, you stayed in. As I said before, when I was out with breast cancer, of all my railroad friends, John was the only one who called.

That didn't make it easier to work together, however, since it put a lot at stake. I had an Irish temper and John was fussy and with the yardmaster getting me riled and John upset, he'd often peel off the engine and go tie brakes while I ranted to the engineer how put upon we were by something or other. Then John would call me at midnight after I got home and go over it all, move by move.

"John," I'd say, "I have to get some sleep," but by then the monologue button would be on and I'd just hope the Viet Nam induction tape wasn't playing, or the rattlesnake-handling-as-a-child tape, or the logging-days tape, and eventually we would hang up and tomorrow would be another day.

After beans we would get our train together, hang a marker, make an air brake test, and head out for the Lawrence district to dodge the commutes. One of us would ride the shove out and we would duck into the butter-house spur. I usually let John go pull the paper-house boxcars while I waited at the main line switch. We would trade out empties for loads on the main, put our drag back together, and John would get on the point to spot the loads at the dock, leaving the butter-house tanks on the lead. I stayed behind to close up the main line switches, report us clear of the main, and line us up for the butter house on the reverse shove. I then walked down to the butter house to line us in and wake up the truck drivers asleep in their cabs parked on top of the tracks.

"See those rails? Well, there's going to be a train on them in about three minutes."

Every night, the same deal. Same truckers, never parked in the clear. Then I'd go inside the factory to get the foreman to pull the blue flag off the pulls so we could couple to them when we came to switch. I usually had the track unflagged and was at the joint when John showed up with the spot cars. We'd then switch the butter house, make the air on our pulls, and shove out to the main line to wait for our chance to get out.

This is where it got exciting for the night. John would walk down the tracks a half mile to the rock-house switch in case we got permission to cross and do our work in the twenty-five-minute window between commutes on the double main line. I waited at the main line butter-house switch and, when the westbound got by, secured permission to get out on the westbound main. Then we moved up to the two pairs of crossover switches and waited for the eastbound.

At this point we usually had about ten cars behind and ahead of the engine. If he was late, we were out of luck and would have to shove back in the clear at the butter house. If he was on time, I could ask the dispatcher for permission to cross over and, if the Mission Bay turn was late and not approaching our block behind the eastbound, he would give it to us. If the Mission Bay turn was out and running, I had to decide whether we still had time to cross over and not stick the next commute. There was about five minutes' wiggle time in our plans.

Sometimes we tried it with less. Then it was rodeo cowboys. John would open a switch behind the Mission Bay to hold a red in the block and I'd get permission to cross. I'd line the two westbound crossovers (sometimes with the aid of a pipe we hid beside the tracks), shove over them, line for the eastbound main, hop on the point, peel off to line the westbound back, hop on again and ride the shove to the rock-house switch at Lawrence. There I would hop off the point car and climb on the engine as it went by, grabbing the 50-pound marker we'd need on our rear and peeling off with it.

Meanwhile I'd watch the shove down to John at the industry, to see that we didn't run over any commuters on the platform. He'd make the hook, ride the rear car out, and peel off to take the shove on the main. We'd leave our pulls on the main, John would ride the point with the spot cars inside, and I would hang the marker on the rear car and go back the main line switch to watch the shove out. John would peel off the last car at the gate, close up, and sprint over to the main to make the couple. I'd send him the cars, close the derail, and report us to the dispatcher as traveling east back to the yard—after our air test, of course.

After a while, we just did our moves without talking to each other, just like old heads. I knew what he was going to do and how long it would take him to do it. We started shaving minutes off our runs. We knew how long each segment of the move took and how long any new problem would add to the sum. Lock wouldn't close, an extra minute at the gate. Stopping to get the marker off the engine and placed near the main line would take another minute. But peeling off on the run with one hand on the grab rail of the engine and another on the 50-pound marker was letting me know I wasn't

20 anymore. That FRED had to go. So I showed up one night with an LED bike light, weighing ounces not pounds, and shaved several minutes off our move. It became our little secret in the yard.

"We noticed your, um, 'marker,'" the conductor on the Mission Bay would say.

"That's what it's for," we'd say, "to get noticed."

All this running made it possible, though not probable, that we could finish up forty minutes early for the night. Not that I could, of course, since I had to do the computer reporting work at the end of the shift, but John could take off for Santa Cruz over the mountain road we drove each day to and from work. We could, that is, if the yardmaster wasn't laying for us when we shoved back to the yard with little jobs to do, moving cars here and there, tidying up the yard. It was the final dramatic moment of the night, whether we would shove down a running track, bleed the cars, kick some into a rail, drop the rest behind them, and go home. Or not. Some final struggle with our Minotaur, the yardmaster who would be there long after we went home and who resented those who wanted to be home and away.

One night he actually blocked John's truck with his company carryall, so that John would have to ask him to move it to escape. John inched his truck forward and back for ten minutes before he extracted it and, of course, called me at midnight to tell me so.

These manly games were wearing me down. I had been plotting my own extraction for years, involving using my other union card, a Ph.D. from Berkeley in English lit. Ever since I wrote my first book on railroad life, in 1990, I had been thinking about teaching college-level literary nonfiction. I had been outside the academy for a long time, and I had a degree in literature, not creative writing. Plus, there were only about four tenure-track job openings in creative nonfiction each year nationwide. My second book, which came out while the merger drama was going on, proved to be the ante in the academic poker game, and I had two job interviews in winter 1998: one in Arizona and another in Georgia. The Georgia job came through.

Wendy was leaving Peter Pan and the lost boys. In June I worked my last day and took a year's leave of absence, knowing I was leaving for good. I gave John the bike light and all my railroad clothes. We wore the same size, and as I mentioned before, he hated shopping. His goodbye present to me was a talking doll he got at Frenchies, the local dirty bookstore. She said, "Me sucky-sucky. Soldier, five dollar. Me so horny. Me love a long time."

I came back to California once and John took me to lunch at a place that had a model train running around the ceiling. I would call him to get the railroad gossip and let him talk on, but there were 2,000 miles between us and we had really only known each other on the job. After a particularly long interval, I left messages but he didn't return the calls.

His brother called me one night to tell me John had gotten home from work one night and dropped dead. His blood alcohol level was lethal. He was 53. His friend Jean told me a little more. New technology in the yard had led to two-man crews, the foreman operating a remote-controlled engine and then doing the paperwork at the end of a twelve-hour shift. The Lawrence job was now even more of a pressure cooker. What an incarceration. He was drinking, she said, when he got home. He'd call her and go over the day. She'd let him talk. He was counting the years to go, seven until he could walk away. He asked for two days off and the UP ran a work history on him. He took them anyway and spent them dead on his floor. As a friend of mine on the Canadian Pacific told me recently, "If you lay off more than one day a month, they start a discipline program against you. If you get ill they want you to take 'family leave act' and go through a ton of paperwork. I know that is not what the authors of the bill had in mind—that the railroad can get out of insurance payments. It's a good thing I like to work."

"John was good at his job," Jean told me, "and he couldn't really do anything else. He liked the railroad work, but the pressure was getting to him of working all alone. John was just everybody's best friend out there."

He certainly was mine, from the first day in July of 1979 until June 1999, twenty years later, when I left it behind. John would have wanted to be remembered as a friend, not as a railroad man. The stories he told, particularly the ones from his logging days, were all about working with people, how he literally worked connections out by handling well his end of a two-man saw, or how working harder and longer forged a bond with people who doubted him at first. One of the last stories he told me was so unlike him in one way, but its ending was pure John.

They were switching the first paper house in the 5 Zone, the one on the wye that abuts on Amtrak's double main line. Of course there's an absolute signal there and the track also slopes down toward it. When he worked with me, John was practically compulsive about tying cars down when he left them and double-checking everything just to make sure. In fact, he nearly drove me nuts with it. But this day he must have been working with some cowboys, because he left some cars on the wye anchored only by a rear car with air, or so he thought. He was just about into the spur when he saw his cut rolling off in the direction of the main line and he started sprinting. He caught the handrail on the last car but didn't have the breath to pull himself up, so he ran alongside it for a while as that big red eye got closer and closer.

"Nobody else could have done this," John told me. He finally hauled himself aboard and cranked them down just feet away from the "Adios, amigo" definition of an absolute signal they told us about in baby brakeman class.

The other absolute was not outrunable. It was not even a danger he recognized. Just something as ordinary as booze, loneliness, and another railroad morning.

THE LORD OF THE NIGHT

When I hired out as a brakeman in Watsonville Junction, California, the Southern Pacific railroad was up for grabs. In 1984, they told us we were going to merge with the Santa Fe, and engines were even painted with combined logos. Conductors in the know showed up with Santa Fe ball caps and uttered statements like "Once John Santa Fe takes over, this kind of crap will cease." Whichever road perceived itself as weaker saw the takeover as Sherman's march to the sea. The railroad unions operate on a seniority system, in which whoever was hired last, the baby, gets last pick of jobs. As a woman and the baby brakeman on the SP road, the speculation and the rumors buffeted me around personally. As it was, I was already cut off every weekend and most of the winter. To try to have some consistent work, I sat out two years of the threatened SP–Santa Fe merger on the safe haven of Amtrak, returning in 1987 after the merger plans fell through.

The next railroad to want the SP was the Denver & Rio Grande Western, who bought it in Santa Fe's fire sale in 1988. We all learned how to pronounce Rye-o-grand correctly, and the dispatchers were all moved to Denver. D&RGW owner Philip Anschutz kept the SP name and held the railroad for eight rocky years before selling it to the UP. Since our railroad was being gobbled up, the usual rumors were circulating.

"Ever ride in a carryall with a UP crew? Them bastards are afraid to talk. Afraid somebody might turn 'em in. I tell you, the fun's over around here. I'm glad I'm not starting out."

We perceived UP crews as slaving under a big brother system wherein even jokes could get you fired. Not that our railroad hadn't participated in this trend toward grim drudgery. When I first hired out in 1979, switchmen seemed to be having so much fun at work they rarely went home. Each shanty had a barbeque out back, and there were hideouts in the districts where card games went on, and pints in paper bags were rites of passage with new hires, to see if you were an informer. Crews routinely hid out in district shanties for a few hours of early morning shut-eye after finishing up district work. They pulled out sheets of cardboard stashed behind lockers and in a few minutes the blackened room would be filled with snores. Just in time for two hours OT, the crew would wake up and complete their last "go home" move before returning to the yard. Not that this system was anarchy. The crews used their skill to do the work fast, but they had control of their own pace. They weren't going to run for ten hours. They would run for five, sleep three, and steal two. This gave them a sense of control over their own lives and the human satisfaction of beating the system in some way. Company officers reached détente with the crews, sometimes cracking down, sometimes loosening up. The bottom line was getting the work done safely, and a good officer just held out for that. In the meantime, the yard was a happening place to be.

Downsizing hit this system hard. With hand-held radios, crew size shrank to two from five. Support personnel disappeared—clerks, roundhouse crews, maintenance-of-way crews, special agents (company police), crew-callers, dispatchers. They all became centralized and thus depersonalized. You no longer knew them and they no longer knew you or your territory. Your switch list was all numbers on a computer screen, and numbers are easy to move around, unlike boxcars. Yards emptied out and the homeless moved in. Brakemen started getting mugged at work by transients. Communication with centralized dispatchers suffered and traffic snarled as crews were called to sit for twelve hours on parked trains. Around 1990, the SP decided to replace paper with hand-held "grid pads" from Tandy, early devices that weren't up to the job. On the grid pad screen, whole blocks of train information disappeared or were garbled. Your train list might or might not resemble what you actually had. Yardmasters yelled at you to go anyway.

Working for the railroad at that time, even though the chaos was throwing me from El Paso to LA on twenty-day stands, I did feel the railroad was giving me something. Self-respect or no respect was my mantra. I liked the challenge of using ingenuity and initiative. I saw myself as the one getting the freight through, no matter what. The strength of the craft provided all the necessary incentive to work up to snuff. On the ground, train crews had the crucial information and it was always the conductor's decision to take the train or make a stand. Company officers stayed out of the way so crews could get the work done. Only during slow times would they hide in the bushes to observe rule violations, and then only after making sure a warning was in the rumor mill. I have since come to understand that self-respect is a rare thing and a quality that is in short supply in most jobs people have to put up with.

Union Pacific took over in September 1996. Our union contract did away with the system seniority that allowed trainmen the freedom to work anywhere on the railroad. As the baby brakeman for so long, I had used this freedom to work from Texas to Oregon, and what I felt now was the loss of all those runs through the beauty of the West. It felt like the end of cattle drives or the buffalo. My Wild West railroad dream was ending.

The UP's first official communication was a little booklet on discipline, arriving in the mail, the company's version of a letter bomb. It was called *Upgrade Policy,* and it had a Germanic organizational quality. There were three columns: the rule violation, the level, and the discipline. The railroad book of operating rules was an imposing tome consisting of rules you absolutely had to follow or disaster would result, rules that were good safety practices, and rules that company lawyers had inserted to protect the company from lawsuits (such as "Don't step into holes"). The rules were frequently amended in timetables and timetable bulletins, which crews had to review each day upon reporting for work. It was a common belief that 100 percent rules compliance would shut the railroad down, and in fact, switchmen threatening such compliance were often targeted for discipline by management. When the company demanded compliance, it was seen as an excuse to fire someone.

In the UP pamphlet, levels of offenses went from 1 to 5. Demerits accumulated for varying periods of time, some vanishing after six months, others persisting for years. Punishments included letters of reprimand, days off without pay from five to sixty, rules exams, corrective action plans. At level 5 the punishment was "permanent dismissal," and level 5 could be reached through addition. In other words, a sufficient number of minor mishaps could get you fired. Most ominously, a personal injury resulted in the next level. (One of the most reprehensible unwritten policies on all railroads was discouraging the reporting of personal injuries because the companies were accountable for these to the feds.) A far cry from the usual response of the Southern Pacific trainmaster who hired me, who would just say, "Oh hell," before he went out and fixed whatever had gone wrong.

Southern Pacific's attitude was that if you weren't having the occasional mishap, you weren't out doing the work. Considering the track and yard conditions on SP (and on UP now), that assessment was pretty much true. "Insubordination," by the way, was a level 5. Well, I guess there wouldn't be any comments to fat trainmasters such as, "When was the last time you saw yer dick?" Such repartee was the norm on the Southern Pacific.

I am sure everyone receiving the pamphlet did what I did. I thought about what I was asked to do every day at work and counted up the unavoidable offenses involved. After one day of normal work, I risked "permanent dismissal." This was just doing what yardmasters told me to do to get the show on the road. "Well," I thought, "if I don't do anything, I can't do anything wrong." It seemed like everyone had this same idea. Suddenly, traffic came to a dead halt and the Union Pacific was into its 1996 legendary great service breakdown.

Well, perhaps the pamphlet was not the sole cause. UP also fired any manager who knew anything about the big operations picture and started closing yards and routes to cut costs, the same yards and routes SP under Anschutz had tried closing before. Predictably, traffic came to a standstill. Hunkered down as I was in the small switching yard in San Jose, I gave thanks that I'd taken the one-third cut in pay to get restricted to the yard to try to recover. Train crews out on the road were getting out on their rest to put in twelve-hour days with no days off. Spouses of trainmen were forming organizations to protest the effect constant around-the-clock work was having on family life. I had worked that way during boom times in Texas and Arizona and I knew I couldn't do it now, after chemotherapy and radiation. The right side of my chest was tight with fried muscles. I discovered I could regain range of motion by throwing ballast rocks, so that was my form of physical therapy, and, since the San Jose yard had no midnight shift, I could at least sleep at night. Out on the main line, the merger chaos would have eaten me alive.

Flying to Tucson in October 1996, I saw train after train parked in sidings. I had worked these lines on our system seniority. I knew what the picture meant. The classification yards were filled up and no traffic could enter them. Train crews were called in the hope that the big red eye on the signal would go green in twelve hours. It never did. So another crew was called to sit. Of course, with the discipline packet in the mail, crews were disinclined to violate any safety rules whatsoever to get trains moving. By the time the Federal Railroad Administration had identified an arrogant corporate culture at UP as a major cause of the breakdown, it wasn't telling us anything we didn't already know.

"I know you're tired," Jolene Molitoris told me. "I know you're overworked."

I was watching her on a videocassette that arrived in the mail in October 1996. She was the head of the FRA and they sent the cassette to every UP operating person. In July 1997, UP sent us all a letter, too, ostensibly apologizing for its errors, but the letter really was a thinly disguised threat not to lay off on weekends. A year later, UP sent along a book by Dr. Nigel Ball, entitled *The Sleep Solution: A 21-Night Program for Restful Sleep.* This was UP's concept of addressing the issue of worker fatigue. Of course, this book was meant to address the problems of people who, given a normal schedule, still can't sleep. Tips for people working shifts didn't really apply to us either, since yard workers were being called ahead of shifts and essentially working eight-on eight-off around the clock. Our problem was, of course, that UP would not let us sleep. In fact, UP interrupted our sleep after six hours and told us to go back to work. Reading their book about "getting out of bed and doing something mildly boring" was not going to do the trick. Like nearly every official communication from UP, it was even insulting.

"If they spent half the money they spend on their slick magazines on fixing the toilets, maybe I wouldn't have to pee in the wind every trip," engineers would grumble.

Trickledown economics wasn't making it to the switchmen's shanty in the San Jose yard. We still had the same old funky railroad and the same hazardous workplace. Only now we were going to be blamed for any and all mishaps, with company officers microman-aging our every move and dumbing down our craft. UP was treating twenty- and thirty-year employees like potential criminals. The former SP was now the red-headed stepchild who was going to get less opportunity, less justice, and more punishment.

The shift took almost comical forms. Long regarded as kangaroo courts, the company's formal investigations into railroad mishaps now assumed conspiratorial dimensions. A UP maintenance-of-way crew went out to do some work in one of our districts without telling our yardmaster. The crew protected themselves by putting up a portable derail and, supposedly, a red flag in front of it a mile from the work site. Unfortunately, the derail was on the right-hand rail around a curve. When the switchmen on a local, Squeaky and Howard, dropped back from the engine to open some gates and do their work, the engineer, now blind on the curve side, ran over the derail.

Since crews from two different crafts and roads were involved, nobody could cover the incident up, and with UP's draconian discipline policy, the switch crew and the maintenance crew turned into adversaries. Who would take the blame? The SP crew swore there was no red flag. At the investigation, a red flag was produced, but it was mysteriously clean after supposedly being run over by a derailing engine. A UP maintenance supervisor testified that he happened to be driving to work near the location in question earlier in the morning and he had seen the red flag. The SP crew called him a liar. The maintenance-of-way department said it didn't have to talk to any SP yardmasters, anyway.

There had always been an adversarial relationship between company officers and trainmen, but now the hostilities included other UP trainmen and the maintenance crews we normally worked with, not against. An us versus them situation was brewing, and, as a woman, I was not sure if I would be included in the "us," if push came to shove. I was feeling this way because, as a play-within-a-play, I had a little drama of my own going on—harassment by the woman-hating yardmaster I was force-assigned to work under as a foreman. This put me in the sacrificial lamb spot.

I say this because some sacrificial offering seemed necessary. The MOW crew walked, and Howard, Squeaky, and the engineer got level 2. They now had a threat hanging over them. It seemed that with the tension and paranoia, more than the normal number of yard and district fender benders started happening. We all wondered when it was going to be our turn.

For a long time now, ever since I had taken advantage of being cut off the extra board to study Spanish, I had been going to Mexico for vacations. I tried to go somewhere new every time, mainly to explore the folk art and different regions. Actually, it was the railroad that initially motivated me, since the migrants who stowed away on our train were usually from Mexico or Central America. I was now able to read and interpret the spray can graffiti that tag artists left on boxcars and industrial buildings. The message I was getting was that Mexico was closer than you think, particularly living in California.

This year, my goal was to meet up with a shaman in a remote village who used bark paper figures in healing ceremonies. I had found a bark paper cutout book in the government folk art store in Mexico City. Later, I located the small village in the state of Hidalgo where it had come from and researched its use. A village shaman had turned fast-disappearing ceremonies using the cutouts into book form, to preserve them. Some of the figures were beneficent—the seed spirits, which were the shadows cast by plants; others were malevolent—the lords of the night, which were destructive forces of nature. These destructive forces had Spanish characteristics. The seed spirits, for example, had bare feet, whereas the lords wore pointy-toe boots. I, of course, identified company officers as boot-wearing types, particularly the yardmaster. A fleeting thought crossed my mind to ask the shaman for a spell. I wasn't the only one. When the switchmen heard about my plans, the requests came pouring in.

"Can you get him to put a spell on the yardmaster?"

"How about an accident, some voodoo, we could all chip in?"

Once I was in San Pablito, Mexico, however, the shaman turned out to be currently in the roasted chicken business, and in the night, I woke up to see a seed spirit cutout illuminated by the moonlight on the wall of my hotel room. In the morning, I understood that it was a shadow cast by a strange tree with thorns on its trunk outside the window, but still, I was glad it was not the lord of the night. I took it as a good sign, and, abjuring harm, I went back to work. The switchmen were disgusted. Why not even try? I sent one of my bark paper cutouts of the night lord to Leslie in Tucson who, being Pueblo Native American, knew about these matters. A year later, when my turn came to be picked off by UP's discipline and punish, the lord would return.

I wasn't thrilled to be force-assigned to the foreman's spot on the Lawrence switcher. Being the junior switchman on the California coast for years, I was used to jobs that weren't so plum. And, strictly speaking, this job wasn't bad. What made it tough was the difficult yardmaster and my help, a switchman who outranked me but didn't want the responsibility of the foreman's spot. El Loco was a Santa Cruz surfer type, living in his van and eating macrobiotic food that he prepared during break. You just never knew what he was going to do, or not do. We got off to a bad start when I told him to stop putting spikes under the wheels to hold the cars, instead of tying hand brakes. Bottom line: He just wasn't going to work with a woman. And here we were, force-assigned, like an arranged marriage. Of course, he could have bid off the job. I couldn't.

It says a lot about railroad life that during my long career, getting stuck working with someone rarely happened. The best aspect of the job, and the reason you put up with the negatives, was the freedom of the workplace. You were mobile and could bid off a job, leave a terminal through a seniority move, or go on the extra board. Since there was no real workplace supervision by the company, this flexibility kept tensions between personalities under control. The

trend, however, was toward more restriction on trainmen's mobility. Increasingly, you were locked into certain terminals, crafts, and locations. Then the company had to mediate disputes fairly, or there would be trouble.

El Loco and I were headed for trouble one night when he simply stopped following my directions during a switching move. Working the field, he turned off his radio, feigned ignorance, and started making smart-ass remarks. The yardmaster was going to be no help whatsoever, since he hated women switchmen as much as he hated El Loco. Six hours later, around 9 PM, El Loco and I were shoving back into the yard from our district with a bunch of cars to drop into a rail. We were all ready to go home. Instead of just making our normal move into our normal track, the yardmaster ordered us onto another lead for the drop, and after that to set 3 Rail over, since he had a local coming into the yard and wanted some room. It was his typical last move of the night complication.

We made our drop and I sent El Loco with the engine into 3 Rail to couple to it so we could pull it out. I let the cars go by us into 6 Rail on the drop and walked down the lead to check that they rolled in the clear, lining the 3 switch behind me so El Loco could come out. What I forgot about was the bull switch that had to be lined for 3 Rail also.

El Loco got the cars together and sent them out to me, over the 3 switch, which I lined back before telling the hoghead to shove ahead. He did, and since the bull switch was split, two hoppers landed in the dirt right in front of me. Well, that's what happens when you forget a switch and the engineer runs through it.

You would have thought the yard was under attack. Instead of the normal comradely commiseration shown when a fellow switchman messes up, El Loco started freaking out on the radio ("What'd she do now?"), and the yardmaster ran over to yell at me ("Can't you do anything right?") and bark orders about where to put the rest of the cars. It was El Loco's big chance to gaslight me for the remainder of the move ("You sure we're in 5 Rail now?") and the yardmaster's big chance to call the trainmaster and order a pee test. I couldn't help but notice that the trainmaster didn't include the engineer, who had equal responsibility for running through the switch, in any testing.

"OK," I thought, "fine."

What was frosting me, of course, was my role as schoolyard victim, a place the yardmaster had defined for me. As long as I was one of the brothers, I could fight this, but allowing myself to be treated differently was the kiss of death. I was going to defend myself, and the way I went about it drew on my former life as an academic. I knew about many recent incidents in which male switchmen had gotten away with worse mistakes. I could even document them. After all, I was a researcher. The disturbing part of this was that it destroyed years of feeling comradeship at work. But then, comradeship was failing me anyway. After eighteen years of fighting to do this job, and of loving the work, I wasn't going to let anyone take it away.

After the derailment, a helper's spot miraculously opened up on a day job, which I bid in. I was working with my old friend Larry, who was goofy but predictable. A couple of weeks later, though, after fighting rush-hour traffic back to Santa Cruz, where I lived, I was not really surprised to find a certified letter from Union Pacific, asking me to sign for a level 2 rules infraction. In typical railroad style, the trainmaster cited the wrong date for the incident and the wrong rule violation for a switchman. But I knew what he meant. I just wasn't signing for any level 2. Being in reach of permanent dismissal would put me in a vulnerable position with the yardmaster. Besides, it takes two people to run through a switch: the switchman and the engineer.

The truth is, I didn't remember throwing or not throwing the switch. That's the way the job is. If you think about everything you do, you can't do it. You have to trust your habits. Nobody wants or tries to put cars in the dirt, and being worried about it only increases your chances of doing it. That was what was wrong with the whole UP punishment system. It made you less competent, not more. Essentially, it was a tool of intimidation, their version of the lord of the night.

I now had a date for the company formal investigation—my first in eighteen years. In the meantime, I began carrying a camera to work and started a journal. I also started researching gender discrimination and checking out lawyers who specialized in it. They acquainted me with the concept of retaliatory harassment, the point being that harassment is hard to prove, but retaliation is easy. I realized I was going to take UP to the mat. In more venomous moments, I envisioned going to law school so I could devote my life to suing the railroad. If UP officials were going to threaten me for my mistake, I would threaten them for theirs. All those years of putting up with harassment for intruding into their man's world was a bill coming due. Either they were going to treat me like one of the boys, or we were going to war.

My friend John, always ready to believe a conspiracy theory, provided me with lots of corroborating evidence. He had shoved over a derail and through an absolute signal a month before and the trainmaster had pee tested everyone on the crew but hadn't charged anyone. John also came up with photos of the damage done when another switch foreman had pulled some industry cars out with their metal ramps still attached. It looked like a giant can opener had been applied to the cars. Again, no formal investigation. Even after I had been asked to sign for my infraction, Larry, with whom I now worked, put some boxcars on the ground in our district, and the same trainmaster didn't charge him.

"Why didn't he order a pee test?" I asked John later.

"Probably because he knew Larry wouldn't pass it," John said.

I was dimly aware that I was suffering from minority paranoia. My incident had happened in the yard, where things couldn't be easily covered up. "But would they cover something up for me?"

I wondered. "No" was the answer I was coming up with. When Squeaky and Larry dropped a caboose over a maintenance-of-way derail in the yard (a blue flag rule violation), they, too, were charged. I hated to say it, but I felt a little better.

About a week after the first certified letter arrived, I got a second one. This letter was a reprimand for taking too many days off. Unrelated to the investigation, this reprimand nonetheless appeared to me to be a one-two punch. In the first place, I hadn't taken any days off. I figured the source of this inaccuracy was crew management's misreporting of my vacation, which I had called up to correct and even asked the trainmaster to correct. Obviously, he hadn't done it. In grand style, I fired off a certified letter of my own, accusing the company of "retaliatory harassment," persistent gender discrimination, and falsification of my exemplary work history. A week later I got another certified letter, apologizing. Flushed with success, I decided it was time to call in the lord of the night.

When my friend Leslie heard about my troubles, she made a photocopy of the lord of the night with a few significant alterations. The original figure held a machete. Now, it held a copy machine, and Leslie added a text that read, "To protect, not to harm." At this point, she assured me, the lord of the night was empowered to work on papers. She instructed me to bundle the lord of the night with the certified letters "from the destroyers," tie up the bundle with cotton string, and throw the whole wad into a stream. For good measure, I added a few of the yardmaster's switch lists and waded out to sea where Aptos Creek met the Pacific. "Bon voyage," I thought, "you fuckers."

Our griever, Jose Abatao, and I met the morning of the investigation at the Cozy Family Restaurant near the San Jose yard. It was a typical railroader's eating place, with plastic wrap-around booths and middle-aged waitresses who were too overworked to be friendly. Abatao was wearing a sweater and slacks. "Are you nervous?" he asked me. "I know I am."

Abatao had taken photographs of the tracks leading up to the derailment site, including the clear view the engineer had of the switch target. He was going for the shared culpability defense. The engineer, by rule, was required to stop short of a switch not properly lined.

We went into the trainmaster's office to face him and Mike Bullard, another manager. Bullard picked up the papers on the trainmaster's desk and studied them for about five minutes. He then turned off the recording machine and looked at us both.

"Well, I don't really know why we're here. It seems like we're saying you didn't line a switch back and you're saying you thought you did, but maybe you didn't. What are you thinking, Jose?"

"I'm thinking I would have required the engineer to stop short of the switch," Abatao said.

"Well, I think I would, too," Bullard said, glancing at the trainmaster. "I'll tell you what, how about you sign for a level 1, 'not always taking the safe course,' and we're out of here."

"Done deal," I said.

"That was the shortest investigation I have ever been to," Abatao said later.

"It's the lord of the night," I said, "working on papers."

Just to spread around the cheer equally, about a week later El Loco was riding in the company carryall when the yardmaster backed into a building. Never one to let an opportunity pass, El Loco claimed whiplash and the yardmaster found himself signing for a level 1, "not always taking the safe course." The symmetry was pleasing.

After six months, my level 1 disappeared, but I never felt the same about the railroad. While making working conditions even harder, UP had undermined my ability to deal with them. Without firing me, the railroad had, nevertheless, managed to steal my job. Where was it, that job I used to love? I was still keeping my harassment log on the yardmaster, and I knew it was only a matter of time before I picked a legal fight with the company. This idea did not appeal to me. It seemed like a negative direction in life, and even if I won, I would not get my old life back.

The one positive during this time was the appearance, in response to a crew shortage, of a new crop of students, the first in twenty years. After being the baby for all that time, I was glad to see some new candidates for the extra board, but also I was glad to see them because I wanted to teach them my craft. Not everybody felt this way. In fact, hardly anyone did. The students, after all, were a pain in the butt. They slowed you down, and you could forget about going home early if a student was on your crew. Plus, they were always doing goofy things, like turning random angle cocks and throwing switches, even when they weren't sure why they were doing it. The old heads were quick to complain that no extra money was involved in teaching them, and working with them was dangerous. All of that was true, but the rookies looked at you like their lives depended on knowing what you knew. That made me realize I did know something, and it was my turn to pass it along. I understood that I was a teacher—a profession I had left behind to follow the railroad.

We had John McDonald with us on his first student trip to the districts to switch out Granite Rock. Granite shared a storage track with a junkyard, and truck drivers were always leaving their vans parked too close, so we warned him to make sure there were no obstructions on the track. He hopped on the point with a radio and rode into the spur to stop the movement before the bumper. We heard him giving car counts and the final "that will do." When he walked back out, we saw that his jacket had been ripped off his back. One of the trailers had been left too close, and he just kept on riding the side of the car. He didn't know enough to judge it or maybe he was too afraid to stop the movement. "You could have been dead," we told him. I could see in his eyes that he got it. He was going to be a good brakeman.

When I took that teaching job in Georgia in August, throwing my switchman's boots out the car window somewhere around Las Vegas, I had managed to leave on my own terms. The only leftover from the railroad was a main line that ran in back of my house in Georgia, carefully chosen so I could hear the wheels rocking the welded rail while I sat in my hot tub and listened.

HOBO. TEHACHAPI, CALIFORNIA (EAST OF).

My last day on the railroad, a photographer from the Santa Cruz *Sentinel* showed up to take pictures. My year's leave of absence was a safety net so that if I couldn't stand the academic life, I could always return. My friend Donna agreed to drive with me across the country, while my earthly possessions remained in storage in Santa Cruz. Since she is an art historian and had given me a life-sized poster of John Wayne, by way of commentary on my railroad personality, I thought it would be fun to photograph us with John at various points on the journey. Donna and I are posing with John in an LA boutique, overlooking Palo Duro Canyon, at the Cadillac Ranch in Amarillo, at my friend Patty's Mexican restaurant in Fayetteville, Arkansas, at the Catfish House in Memphis, and finally on the golf course in Marietta, Georgia.

In Georgia, I found the home I had been looking for, a home predicted by the train rug in Gallup that Donna and I saw in a roadside trading post, the kind my family always visited in their long car trips coast to coast. The weaver used the sacred mountains as a horizon and a hogan for the center. Locomotives represented the four directions. Around the hogan clustered sheep, horses, a pickup truck, and corn. The CSX main line ran north and south behind the Victorian cottage I bought in Georgia. Actually, this was the reason I bought the house. My life centered on my home. School was only a ten-minute drive. I was pleased to learn that Atlanta was formerly called Terminus—where the railroad ended.

The fifty trains a day over the main line seemed to be coming directly through my house, but eventually I didn't hear them unless I wanted to. They became dream trains, as I got used to the luxury of sleeping nights. I had no longing to be on any of those trains, but it kept that part of my past alive for me. In the university world, I soon discovered, only words mattered, whereas on the rails, you were judged by actions and every day was a new day. I made the transition to working inside by planting seventy-seven trees and shrubs my first year there, using a Mattock pick to create the planting holes in the Georgia red clay soil. As tired as I used to be from a day on the rails, I would fall into bed and listen to the trains blow the five crossings of the Marietta Square. Only the night local made me want to come near.

One rainy Sunday night I heard the continuous motion stop. The engine idled for a few moments, snorting occasionally like a whale, and then, with a big hole release of air it started forward again, slack running out like dominoes. My counterpart, the brakeman, was there in the night, making the cut, climbing aboard the last car, riding to the switch. The night local brought the human presence home, linked the place I lived to the connecting transportation of the running freight—the moments of intense activity that used to be my job, until I got back on the engine and rode to the next industry spot, connecting the dots, making another map, another grid on the landscape I lived in.

They say that whatever you start out doing on the railroad, that's what you miss. For me, it was working local freight in the Salinas Valley of California. I had that job, really, for about four months when I first hired out, before the winter layoff, and the gradual dismemberment of local freight and even the Watsonville yard itself. I came back to it in beet season every year until even that boom time became too hard to hold for the baby on the whole SP system.

Local freight wasn't only about the open window and the world streaming by or the sensation of inevitable weight in motion. It was about the hidden places in the normal world, the off-the-grid adventures you only have as a child, when you climb fences, crawl through ditches, and seek out vacant lots and ramshackle buildings. The local switching tracks take you behind the façade to loading docks and cavernous paper houses, junkyards treacherous with rusty iron, careless traps laid for the switching crew at night, tractor trailers left foul of tracks, switches run through and often impossible to throw, hand brakes bent and rusty, ready to pull your teeth into their whiplash.

Unexpected colors greet you. Industrial found art. The monstrosity of containers, painted shocking orange, chartreuse, bright blue. Oversized yellow spools, mountains of green crushed plastic, hills of brown glass. In the mine jobs out of Tucson, gondola cars filled with copper ingots, each the size of a double door, wealth out of the earth, smelted and gleaming. Oversized industrial parts for machines, taking the space of an entire flatcar, tied down with yellow cord. Space-age materials in muted greys, weird geometric shapes. A playground for the mind. Inside warehouses, tin can stacks the size of buildings, forty-foot tanks of butter, walls of tires. In Salinas, conveyor belts dripping green, smells of rotting broccoli, hoses shooting ice. Clouds of chocolate hanging over Spreckles, the cacao nibs left on the floor of boxcars, sweetness in the very air. A river of fire down the slagheap in El Paso, white orange against the black.

I did not know that hidden world in Georgia, where I had neither been a child nor worked on the railroad. But thanks to the railroad, I knew that it existed.

Thanks to the railroad, I was unafraid of the dark. One of my neighbors, bless her heart, came over to welcome me.

"I came home late one night and I didn't want to walk to my door in the dark, so I called the Marietta police and those gentlemen came and escorted me."

I pictured the woman huddled in her car, just feet away from her house, phoning the police. "OK," I thought. "Fine."

Not all my neighbors were so timid. One morning at 3 AM I awoke to a wall of fire just a hundred yards across the street. A house under renovation was burning to the ground. The developer blamed the evicted tenant. A year later, my neighbor across the street, the only person friendly enough to invite me to dinner, shot himself and his two young children, over a divorce. I pictured him in his upstairs room, his state of mind. Why didn't he walk across the street and say something? I could practically see the room it happened in. This was suburbia, for God's sake. Not some wasteland on the border. My blessing was that I had sacred datura living with me, from California cuttings a friend had brought with her on a visit. The week of the suicide, the datura burst into yellow bloom, filling the house with its nocturnal perfume. The tree kept blooming for the entire month, like a friend who called every day.

"Medea," I told my students, "lived next door to me. This may be an old story, but it happens here, too." They just stared at me, the way they usually did, counting time.

I wasn't prepared to face a room full of eyeballs staring at me. The classes I came to Georgia to teach, writing life stories, were fun right from the start, but the composition classes they saddled me with were another story. My last experience in college, during the sixties, assumed a literate society. That much had changed. Few students could read a paragraph from a dense literary text. They universally hated writing. After a few years, I figured out how to teach them, but at first I seriously thought about going back to railroading. The house itself kept me there, as the train rug foretold. I had wanted it for so long, I just kept working on it and mastering my new craft until I had a new world I could live in.

I will always be a rail. Ironically, it wasn't until I went to Springfield, Illinois, to read to a legislative convention for the United Transportation Union, that a fellow railroader called me "brother." I was crossing the lobby, the morning after the reading, and he addressed me that way. It meant a lot, mainly that through the writing, I could still be in the railroad world and say something meaningful to my fellows. Rails can't really talk about their work to people in the outside world. I have already mentioned the problems with doctors, but people with regular hours regard those who don't have them as unreliable, since they often can't keep appointments. Actually, the opposite is true. A rail will get up in the middle of the night when her beeper goes off, in the middle of a storm, and drive an hour to work somewhere she has never been, and then work twelve hours if she has to, and then drive home. Without complaint. Year in and year out. The first thing I noticed about my students was how even a little rain often kept them home from class.

"It's not raining in here," I would say, peevishly.

If it snowed, the whole school would shut down. Any inconvenience was enough to make them give up. I wondered how they planned to work the rest of their lives.

"I don't need to know grammar," a student told me. "I'm going to have a secretary to do that."

"In your dreams," I thought. Actually, people in India handle all jobs requiring grammar. I don't know where that student and his secretary are going to work.

The railroad gave me a working-class consciousness. Immigrants still had it, but the society around me all wanted to be dot-com entrepreneurs, living on credit. They all drove much better rides than I did, but at least mine was paid for. Once, at a reading at Georgia's military college, a student came up to me and asked how hard it was to be a writer.

"Well," I said, "you can probably have what's first on your list. If you want to be a writer, you can do that. If you want to have a house and car and cell phone and flat screen TV, you can probably do that."

She looked like she got it.

The culture in Georgia was non-union and fundamentalist religious. People seemed to believe in individualism, at all costs. The railroad taught me differently. Anything emanating from the company and by extension, the government, was propaganda. I respected the people I worked with and learned that I needed to communally defend our integrity and our working conditions. The company did not have our interests at heart in any way, in spite of the fact that we served them well and honorably. We learned to always look a gift horse in the mouth. A case in point would be the watches the company handed out for not reporting an injury for a year. This did not mean you didn't have an injury, only that you did not report one. The reason for this? Reporting injuries had negative consequences for the railroad. Rather than spend money fixing a hazardous physical plant, they handed out trinkets.

The whole drift in worker/management relations was toward cutting costs and blaming the worker for anything that went wrong. The cult of individualism plays into this scheme. Historically, the railroad was required to institute its own system of insurance (Federal Employers Liability Act—FELA) because its workplace was recognized to be exceptionally hazardous. A private insurance company could not be expected to insure against such inherent risks. Well, the workplace is the same, but now the workers, individually, are responsible for all hazards? Unlikely and ahistorical, but consultant companies are busy marketing the idea under the rubric of "Total Safety Culture." A win-win situation for everybody but the workers.

No wonder I was glad to see the Mexicans lining up for work at my corner drive-in. They had at least one revolution in recent history. Perhaps they would eventually turn the tide here.

I'm always on time, to the minute. I still have everything I need in my truck for a week on the road. I am afraid of telephones, including cells. I think a voice on the phone is going to tell me to get up and go to work. My nightmares re-enact these call backs. I don't want to be reachable. The ability to sign up for dance classes and make appointments I can keep seems like a wonderful luxury to me. My health is better; chronic sinus problems have gone away and I have not had a recurrence of cancer. I think the main thing I have taken away is that I want good work. I want to work doing something that serves the community and I want to be effective. I want to see results that are similar to switching out a yard full of boxcars or taking a train from point A to point B. I can't accept too many mistakes and if I make them, I expect to pay for them, not find a way to pawn them off on other people. The process of buying a house shocked me because my agent kept making mistake after mistake, all of which I paid for. This is routine in an office environment. The customer is supposed to regroup and try again. Slough off everything on the consumer and if a consequence comes around, blame the employee. No use complaining to the voice on the phone. That person is either under the gun or in India or both. I guess I don't see the vision in how our society works. How can a society keep working this way? The railroad world I hired into in 1979 was a world unto itself, but as such it made sense. The craft was everything and you paid dues learning it and proving yourself. Then you could practice it for thirty years and win a decent living. Rewards were instantaneous and punishments were severe, injury to yourself or people you cared about. The work ethic policed itself.

By deskilling the craft and demoralizing the workforce, management thinks it can deal out punishment and reward. That will never happen. People don't work just for money, and if they did, they would never choose to work on the railroad. It's just too hard. My students can barely bestir themselves to come to class. They're not going to get up at 3 in the morning and work in the rain. Immigrants might do it, but we are busy criminalizing them. Well, now that I am living in the world of ideas, as opposed to, as my foreman in El Paso put it, "the world of men," I have plenty to think about.

WAITING FOR THE TRAIN. TEHACHAPI, CALIFORNIA.

19 THE SPIRITUAL BEAUTY OF THE RAILS

Be the current against us, what matters it? Be it in our favor, we are carried hence, to what place or for what purpose? Our plan of the whole voyage is so insignificant that it matters little, maybe whither we go, for the "grace of a day" is the same! Is it not a recognition of this which makes the old sailor happy, though in the storm; and hopeful even on a plank out in mid-ocean? Surely it is this! For the spiritual beauty of the sea, absorbing man's soul, permits of no infidels on its boundless expanse.

JOSHUA SLOCUM, *Voyage of the Liberdade*

Joshua Slocum, the captain and boat builder who sailed alone around the world, writes about the "spiritual beauty" of being at the mercy of the ocean. Slocum built a perfectly balanced sloop that would hold its course with no one at the helm. He knew how to navigate, using only a dollar alarm clock, and made every one of his landfalls. He even renounced killing fish, not wanting to harm another creature, eating only the flying fish that brained themselves on his mast. He repelled boarders using only carpet tacks. He welcomed accident, seeing in it a partner for his own readiness. Railroading has a similar beauty, since you never know what any day will bring or how you will react to it.

Old railroad songs warn wives not to quarrel with their husbands, for the wives don't know if they will ever see their husbands again. Holding on to the grab irons doing the brakeman's work is the furthest extension of this vulnerability, since it only takes a lost hold to fall beneath the wheels. As I write these words, I remember Tom Mace, who lost his hold untying a high brake on the Lompoc job. He was rolling by a track when he heard a brake. By the rules, he should have stopped the motion, located the brake, and untied it. But nobody works that way. He heard the brake, swung aboard, and untied it. Then he lost his hold. Nobody wanted to talk about that night.

The wreck of the Old 382 might have claimed Casey Jones, but a normal everyday error can take the life of a brakeman. Reading through the Federal Railroad Administration's yearly accident report one time, I saw that no matter how much experience a trainman had, it was easy to fall off or get hit by moving equipment unawares. If you know any day such a fate might happen to you, riding on the side of a boxcar inches from the wheels, you experience life differently than those who believe themselves safe. Only other rails understood this. Railroad life was outside the ken of just about every middle-class person, the group I used to belong to.

The spiritual beauty of the railroad was exiting the freeway on which I assumed things were going to be a certain way, or where I had the luxury of testing limits, onto another road, where long heavy objects were in motion from Maine to California, all day and all night, their trajectory running through every location and enterprise the daytime world engaged in. From the train, I saw Saturday night couples drinking wine. I saw their suburbs empty on Monday afternoons, their long lines of gridlock, and at other times, freeways empty enough to skateboard on. The train uncovered, attracted even, the secret economy of migrant workers, living beside the tracks, and the addicted and homeless in their makeshift shelters. We dodged winos and junkies and yuppies in Lycra biking suits, office workers running for a commute, those who despaired and took their own lives in front of our train and those who just stupidly did so, wearing Walkmans while jogging between the rails.

I knew a thin permeable membrane separated the predictable world from the chaotic one; I crossed it nightly and returned home thankful that home was there. The spiritual beauty of the rails required that I accept this, that I was the wino with her head on the rails, but not tonight.

When I first hired out, my grandmother, bless her heart, really encouraged me. She wanted me to get the job. When I did actually get the job and had to go through the ninety days, she took me to get work boots and my watch. She told me after ninety days that my great-grandfather, a switchman, had been killed in 1947 in Brooklyn yard. I had no knowledge of this, and she didn't want to discourage me from actually trying. She said, "You can do anything you want," and she kept telling me that.

I figure if it's going to happen, it's going to happen. I just I live my life now. Friends of mine have been going 60 mph and the train just jumps the track. I have this thing where I never go to work mad. I've had to lay off on a call before because I was in an argument with my husband, and I just said I can't go to work like this. I never bring in anything else on the job with me. From day one, I've really clarified that because I realize things happen. You hit people in cars, and there are times you need your wits about you. You might have to save someone's life, or I

might be injured and the last thing I remember is fighting with my husband.

I never saw myself as doing what I do until I did it, and then I realized that God really chose this for me. I have a lot of time to commune with my own thoughts; I have a lot of time to read; I've gotten to know myself better than I probably ever could in a job where I constantly have to be thinking about someone else. I have a lot of time to self-reflect when I'm going across the countryside at 6 in the morning and there are hours and hours of just hearing the engine roar. I've been thankful for that all these years. I can't think of anything I would do that I would like better. I can't say what the future holds for me except I enjoy what I'm doing today and I am a very day-to-day person. That's probably why the railroad's so good for me, because it's a new day, every day. You never know when they're going to call you. (Bonnie Susbauer, Southern Pacific conductor)

I went to their doctor for my physical. I think they must have taken twenty back X-rays. The doctor said, "Why would a nice girl like you want to do something like this?"

I said, "Money." It was certainly more money than I had ever made at anything. I had even been a schoolteacher, and I never made money like that.

Just as I was leaving he said, "I want to show you something," and he took me over to the window and held up a slide of this guy's foot that had gotten caught underneath and was run over. It was totally mangled. He said, "I just wanted you to see what you're getting into." (Mary Stevens, Southern Pacific switchman)

Often, only the stories rails tell each other mark an accident. You might hear everything some Hollywood celebrity has for breakfast, but you won't hear about a switchman getting cut in half twenty miles down the highway from where you live. The spot, marked in blood, is immediately obliterated by the railroad, fearing liability.

"He left a debris field behind him," Howard told me. "It got him right above the pelvis. The company rushed over and re-graded the ballast and cleaned up the yard. It was like messing with a crime scene."

The twenty-year gap in hiring is now a chicken coming home to roost. When I left the railroad in 1999, they were just hiring new people. Now the old heads are going, going, gone. There is no one to teach the craft and the craft is being deskilled. No getting on and off moving equipment. No drops or other skilled moves requiring a team.

"You know how it used to be that there were one or two people who were clueless and about a thousand who knew what was going on," Howard said. "Now, it's reversed."

When the UP tore up the San Jose yard, they moved the local switching back to Watsonville, which is a yard with a slight grade, not a bowl. A car will roll so hard from the top end that it will knock the brakes off a heel and send the whole rail out the bottom end. A short crew was working with a remote-controlled engine and kicked a car up a rail from the bottom of the yard. They didn't kick it hard enough, so it started to roll back onto them, and a new hire made the decision to jump on the brake to slow it down before it hit the engine. He missed his hold and ended up underneath the wheels.

My friend Carter, who lives twenty miles down the road and reads the local paper every day, never heard of it. I heard it from a rail. It is part of the history we need to remember and pass on, because we need to know that the earth can open and swallow us.

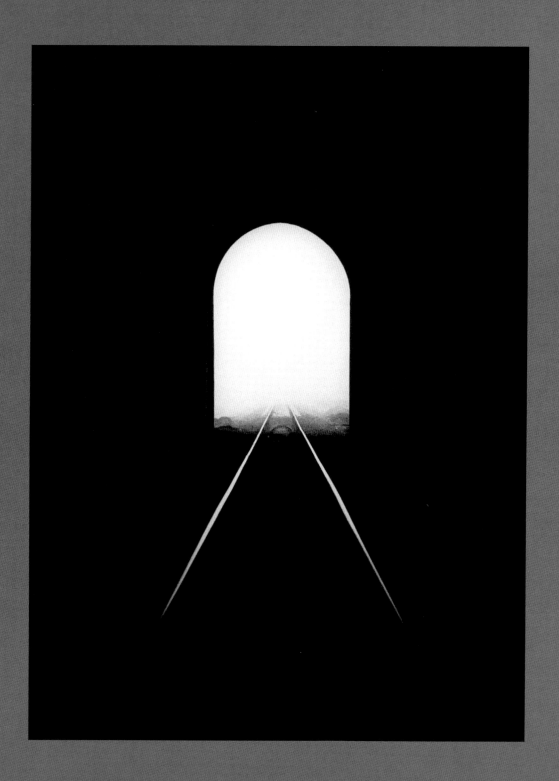

TUNNEL. CAJON PASS, CALIFORNIA.

When I think about the deskilling of the craft, the normalizing of high turnover of workers, the attack on unions and job protection funds, and the blame-the-worker safety programs, I think about the bonds of craft and human satisfaction in life that railroad work used to represent. Surely this way of life is worth fighting for, both in railroading and other walks of life. I would hope it will be there for my successors.

GROUSING

I asked Ceace Poxon, an LA hoghead retired in 2005, about the new hires.

"The ones from the military; they think they know everything. You tell them 'just watch.' The problem is they don't know they're in trouble until it's too late. I tell them the story about the engineer on the big Cajon Pass derailment. He had more weight than he knew and he never came back after that. One new hire ran me through a switch engine window; another one pulled the air on me and I clocked him. He brought me to an investigation and they said, 'She's too little to do that to you.' The thing is they have no respect for the craft, how dangerous it is. How it's like a ballet dance."

Howard Halla, my compañero in the hospital yard, also gave me an earful.

"You wouldn't recognize it," Howard told me. "I have this little speech I give. It's like you're starting over every night. I feel like I'm falling backward into space. You have to tell them the most basic things, like where the clearance point is. Now they have cones set out so they can see. Every night, I'm trying not to get fired because they take the whole crew now. The smartest thing I ever did was to refuse to be promoted."

KEVIN KLEIN

I used to work with Kevin when he was a switchman in Watsonville. For the last eighteen years he has been the general chairperson of the UTU General Committee of Adjustment, fighting the company over claims. I asked him about the training new hires were getting. He told me that the big difference was due to short crews composed of mostly new hires. After a sixteen-week training period of tagging along with a regular crew, the person is often on a short yard crew using remotes or on the road with just an engineer. They learn to use remotes at the end of the training, so that a person with little experience handling cars is then trying to handle a locomotive at the same time.

"I think underlying all this is the effort to deunionize the workforce. They didn't hire people for a fifteen-year gap. Now they shove the old guys out and have these other people completely retrained with their ideas, and I think they're being successful with it. By keeping the new employee away from the old employee, there's no talk of the union. We don't see time claims anymore. That used to be one of our biggest things, but they have neutralized the old folks because they gave them a protective allowance higher than any time claims they could generate. Now they don't bother to do time claims, plus they're not working with a new guy showing him how to do time claims. The new hires, unless they're proactive and want to go to the union and find out, they don't know what to do. We are so buried with discipline. That's all we do."

Kevin told me that the heavy-handed discipline policies have nearly bankrupted the job insurance policies that most people, including myself, never had to use.

"A lot of people thank you for that, now. They want to eliminate all mistakes. Just do things you are capable of doing. And you can't point out to them that the world's been going on a long time and no one has ever eliminated mistakes. You point out the mistakes they make and they don't want to hear it."

The picture I was coming away with from the old heads was of whole crews of new hires stumbling around in the dark, reinventing the craft, trying to follow the step-by-step instructions of company managers, most of whom had never switched out cars. I decided to find some new hires and talk to them. What was their railroad like?

JOEY

Joey showed up to meet me in Santa Cruz in a car that reminded me of what I was driving my first years on the railroad. His beat-up Honda had wood and pinecones on the dash, clothes and a sleeping bag in the back, and evidence of food consumption in the front seat. When I hired out, I drove a '56 Chevy with bald tires that I blew out consecutively driving to the class in Watsonville. Joey himself was

about 25, with impressive tattoos and a compact, athletic body. I felt like telling him to get a vehicle he could sleep in, but I forbore. He looked like he knew what the score was, anyway. He told me that Oakland switchmen had unofficially moved into the old Amtrak building on 16th Street and it was kind of a dorm. Having spent many a night in the back of my truck in that same parking lot, I could picture it.

Bums and switchmen sharing the same space opened up a line of talk that led to his telling me he used to be on the other side, a freight train rider and urban graffiti artist, even as a kid growing up next to a yard and roaming the railroad space as his backyard. He had read all the railroad literature—not that there's a whole lot out there—but myself, Ted Conover, Kerouac. He knew the history of the craft, missed working with the old heads and saw being a switchman as continuing to stay on the edge of legitimacy, skirting the rules, looking for beauty, art, and pride. Looking for something masculine, American, and traditional.

"I went to military school when I was 13 and I remember the same feeling I had about the really Draconian policy in military school. I remember being in class, standing in formation, being yelled at by the sergeant major and hearing about all these new policies they had, and I thought, 'Oh fuck. This is stupid. I can't believe this,' and I feel the same way with the UP and some of the rules they make up. Up in Roseville you have all these khaki-clad business school assholes who've never worked on the railroad, who are trying to do everything by the book.

"On the San Leandro job there were these two brothers. They hired out in '04 but they were schooled totally by the old heads, and they would take this job that would take other people eleven hours and they would get it done in three. They were double-pinning shit. I was a student and I'd been on there for like a month, and he said, 'Just throw these switches.' At first he said, 'Just sit in the engine.' It blew my mind that they were so graceful, so on top of it. They were 29-year-old kids and there would be strings of cars floating down the tracks, and I'm like, 'How are you doing that?' They were not even stopping the engine. That was the first and only time I've ever seen a drop done. On the fucking main. Shit, that would totally have some business asshole in a fit. But they did it. They did it really good. To be able to take pride in their work, that was the big thing for them. I worked with one of the brothers on the job two months later and I said, 'Man, you guys blew my mind when you did that, just seeing you work like that,' and he said, 'Yeah, we got schooled by all these old heads.' He said this stuff that I thought was kind of cheesy, but it really made sense. He said, 'You can feel like a man.' It sounds like macho shit, but what he was saying was you can take pride. It was this totally badass deal that takes skill and confidence and having the right feel for it.

"I respect this job. It does affect you. There's no way to not feel emotionally tied to something you're losing sleep over, and you find ways to get around the rules. You find the loopholes and when management's not watching, you can get stuff done. All this Safety Culture hogwash can be thrown out the window. Of course, who wants to get hurt or hurt anyone else, but it's about being able to do a job and do it good and not fuck up equipment. The craft's been around for 150 years. I don't like patriotism, but I think there's something really American in that. It's totally about pride, but not a mega sense of pride, not hubris. I doubt that accountants have this sense of pride. After having your ass kicked by the job, like working in the rain or being cold as hell, or being out there for twelve hours, there's no way that it can't become a part of you. You know, like, 'I went through this shit storm but I totally feel good about it.'

"The UP shoots itself in the foot with the relationship between management and employees. I mean, this is a job where morale could be good. They wouldn't have shit to worry about. Stuff probably wouldn't get messed up. People wouldn't lay off so much, and people would be allowed to take more pride in their job instead of being harassed by all this bullshit. I do want to say safety is important, but after a while, I don't need to be told how to walk. You hear

what it was like to work for SP. There was bullshit but not in such huge dump truck loads. The hiding out in the bushes—there's no need for this. I had an old Western Pacific guy in Milpitas tell me that trainmasters would hang out in the crew shack playing cards with us—like everyone had the same goal, getting these trains out on time. They took pride in being fucking trainmen.

"I miss railroad smarts. What if I need to know how to do stuff and it's lost? It seems like there have been so many badass people, really solid molded people, like back then, 'Cars were made out of wood, men were made out of steel.' I'm like, 'Give me a break.' But they were that caliber. This old head the Commodore was funny. His whole attitude and demeanor was calm. It was great to be around him. He was hilarious. I remember him saying, 'I got my name when I put two engines in the Brazos. Two huge engines fell in the river. There goes one.'"

JEN WALLIS

Seattle in September was blowing a 40 mph gale when I flew in. I always forget the scale of the northwest—the looming Cascades, glimpses of the giant bay as you wind up the streets, the working port with cranes like orange toys, the ships coming in and out. It made San Francisco look like miniature golf. I was here to talk with Jen Wallis, a switchman on the Burlington Northern. Jen had written me after reading *Boomer* and offered up as a bona fide the blog she created while walking from Seattle to Washington, D.C., "collecting grievances." I was intrigued.

The walk grew out of the World Trade Organization police riot in Seattle in 1994. Jen was working downtown at a typical office job and was out at lunchtime. She was swept up in a crowd she could not escape from, teargassed, and arrested. A military brat who had to sacrifice as a child, she was outraged that something like this could happen to a citizen. She remembered not having her nuclear submarine father home for Christmas, the constant moving around, standing at attention for taps every day, being the new kid in schools all the time.

"I thought, I'm sorry, but this happens in other countries," she said. "In this country it happens to bad people. It doesn't happen to good people."

In jail she met a lot more good people and soon found herself on longshoremen's picket lines and at organizing meetings around Seattle. But after a few years, meetings were wearing her down. She is an action type of person. Then something magical happened, starting with getting stung by a bee.

"When I got stung by the bee, I broke out in hives. I had some Benadryl with me and I drove myself to the ER. Standing in line, my throat closed up and I was finding it difficult to breathe, and then I passed out and the next thing I knew I woke up. It took three shots of epinephrine to bring me around, and it was really serious. When I came out of that, I just thought, 'Oh, how precious life is. It is so short and I don't want to die like that. I want to die doing something huge.' When I had that calling, I thought, 'I have to do it because I've had this experience (as a military child) and I love my country and I would die for it.' I really thought I was going to die on the walk. And then, after I was dead, people would hear about it. And that was a good thing. I was resigned to it. In the back of my mind I was waiting to get shot, and it never happened."

On September 11, 2001, she was camping in Utah, after losing support team members who came to realize her publicity campaign was not going to smooth the way. She realized that this was not the moment to be alone on the road, with an infected blister and a sign that said "5,000 miles on foot for democracy." She returned to Seattle for the winter and resumed her trek April 1, 2002—one year to the day after she started. She met a lot of ordinary Americans who fed and sheltered her and Sherpa, her dog. She talked with them about democracy and how to get involved in it. She learned that a lot of working people were just getting by.

"People were buying groceries from the dollar store," she said.

Washington on June 13, 2003, seemed anticlimactic. She took a look at the outside of the White House and quietly bought a van and started to drive home. With her was "Baltimore Red," a sometime railroad worker, sometime freight train rider, and longtime Wobbly. In Dillon, Montana, they parked the van and Red showed Jen how to catch out on a train, the Dillon local that ran to Silver Bow. The ride was glorious—July weather, the Big Hole River running along the tracks, clouds moving on their own river of rails above them. They ran through farmland, desert, mountains, and ranching country. Local signage informed them they were in John Wayne country. It was a reward for the slow travel by foot, the trudging. Riding in boxcars and in the third unit on engines, they saw America the beautiful that few citizens get to see. As Ted Conover has commented, only the hobos and railroaders really know the country end to end. It was a fitting reward for a patriot. And here Jen got the idea of what she would do when she got back to Seattle—hire out on the railroad, which she did.

"I mostly followed old railroad tracks," she told me, "into the little towns."

Jen saw the railroad as another opportunity for grassroots organizing. One of her heroes was Mother Jones, who she first read on the walk, the book a gift from the Chicago Wobblies.

"I never really felt like I had anything to be proud of, in terms of class and race, being a white cracker girl from Texas, but then when I read about being a part of the working class, I had this realization that I belong to something. I felt like I could identify for the first time and be proud of the culture."

The first few years on the railroad were discouraging.

"My first job out of Stacy yard was with a couple of old head women and I thought 'Oh, this is going to be so fun,' and they just scowled at me, and that whole night, they just ran me into the ground. I would be standing on the deck and she would be five feet from the switch and she would get on the radio and say, 'Come throw the switch,' and the engineer was yelling at me because I wasn't getting off on the other side of the cab, and it was so awful. We were shoving into a track and I noticed one of the tracks started rolling and was going to roll right into the locomotive, and I told her but she didn't stop. So I ran over and tied the brake real fast on the car and tied another brake and I got it stopped, and afterward in the yard office at the end of the night, they said, 'Hey, you did a good job; you did real well out there.' And I thought, 'You were so mean to me. What was that all about?' 'Oh well,' they said, 'it's so hard training new people. You get so tired.' But that is about the meanest experience that I had on my career on the ground. That was my first day. No one really showed me anything. They assumed you had been trained, but I didn't know what to do with a list."

Once footloose, now Jen has a 3-year-old son and a mortgage. She has settled down as much as a railroader can. Still an activist, she joined a wildcat union called Railroad Workers United, which is a pressure group for worker unity. Railroaders need each other now, for information as much as anything else. The old heads aren't around to teach them and the UTU is busy defending disciplinary cases. The internet makes this type of organizing much easier than depending on railroaders to show up at a physical meeting place.

"I give people the Railroad Workers United newsletters; they roll them up, put them in their pocket, and that's it. I've never had a discussion based on one of the articles. I don't get that. I think it's part of the mentality. They are too tired out to make sense. I would bake cookies and leave them out, and when I left the room they would just suck them up. There would be no thank you, nothing like that.

"There are so many trainmasters. What do they do? I don't know. They have a quota they have to fill. Some of them sit in the office and put on the computer all kinds of things like alcohol on the breath and you never talked to the guy. They have a little camera scanning the yard that works at night. They have no idea why we sit in the yard office for an hour. I think there is definitely a plan on the part of the railroads to get rid of the union, somehow. They have a plan and we don't. These things harden you. They make you resentful. But, it's like the walk. I take these things and turn them into something positive. Get that anger and put it toward something I'm going to do. Union organizing. And I think it's different to have that. The first year there was nobody listening."

JOE WYMAN

Joe Wyman hired out on the UP in 2006 and already had a booming story similar to mine. Marking up in Las Vegas, Nevada, he was soon cut off. He then transferred to El Paso but was cut off before he got there. He then did a seniority swap to Tucson and is now seven months into another furlough. When the UP tried to implement Total Safety Culture in Tucson, Joe led the union fight against it and won.

"I was the one who threw the stone at the hornet's nest and I was the one who kept throwing stones while getting stung. When I came home that afternoon after giving the initial RWU presentation, there was a threatening phone call on my answering machine. Someone used the voice changer. Scary? Yes, but affirming because what it said was that we had hit a nerve. It told me we were really on track. Fundamentally, the reason I fought it so hard is I don't want to sit in an emergency room with someone, someone's spouse or son, or mother, after this program gets in and they get killed or injured because of it. It's like a rabid dog. You don't want to let this into your house."

The program is a product marketed to large companies by Safety Performance Solutions, a consulting firm. It emphasizes individual responsibility for safety. The following are the bullet points on TSC from their webpage:

1. Safety is held as a value by all employees.
2. Each individual feels a sense of responsibility for the safety of their coworkers as well as themselves.

3. Each individual is willing and able to "go beyond the call-of-duty" on behalf of the safety of others.
4. Each individual routinely performs actively caring and/or safety behaviors for the benefit of others.

The program recruits employees to observe fellow employees and rate their safety performance ("The key to this safety process is the Behavioral Observation and Feedback Process"). Employees who buy in are given certain perks. Joe's problem with this rhetoric is that it ignores the elimination of workplace hazards, the very thing that FELA was enacted to address. My problem with it is that it is insulting, as if railroaders didn't already look after each other.

"It leads to less reportables, and it has a union-busting component because it co-opts union members and degrades solidarity, and in American culture no one likes a rat. What we want is a union-based, union-controlled safety program that has the health, safety, and wellness of our members as the whole main goal and the only concern without any ulterior motive. Look at the track record. It would be one thing to say, 'Look, this thing came in and the intimidation has stopped, the injury discipline has stopped,' but we know there is a de facto injury discipline policy. If the company can say that 'you went through the safety program so now you're safe and we have all these people watching out for you to make sure you are safe,' they can say, 'Now you're hurt; it must be your fault.' Injuries happen in the workplace because of exposure to hazards.

"What it showed is they didn't shove it down our throat. We said no to it. And we forced them to the table. That's really a pretty big deal. An article by Fred Gamst, an anthropologist, talks about how TSC never takes a look at the latent problems that exist that start on the drawing board or in the boardroom with policy and infrastructure. My only goal is to have real safety. Out there, they say it's not dangerous, it's unforgiving. Well, it is dangerous. Yes, there is no excuse for someone who is going to act unsafely and not follow safety rules. You can't do that and if you're going to do that, you're

in the wrong job. You should follow procedures, but despite that, even when you do that, the machines we work around and the work environment need to be built around us. I saw this picture years ago of a freight car in some European country and the bottom rung, which would be a ladder for us, was a, just a nice little steel plate, comfortable to stand on. Just think of the added safety of just that little plate to stand on instead of hanging out. Real design change is all about money. To increase real safety in our workplace will cost a lot more money than these programs.

"A couple of my union brothers on the safety committee have been meeting with the company and for more than two years they have been asking for ballast between main 1 and main 2 here. When they did some work several years ago, they didn't think to make it so you could walk between the two mains. We have been asking for this because it's treacherous. Just recently, it got done and this Total Safety Program got credit for it. So here's what you're saying to us. For two years the safety committee has been meeting with someone who hasn't listened to anything they said, and now you're going to tell us because of Total Safety Culture and this behavior-based safety program—that's what got this done? Was it not a safety issue before and now it is? Why are you listening to it now and you weren't before?

"Tomorrow railroad executives can flip the switch and have non-agreement employees running our trains. The goal is to have computers running the train, to have no employees. We need people working jobs from a humanistic standpoint. People need jobs. Can you imagine being an engineer out there on your own, and when it's time to go do your work, you leave the cab and you grab your remote control box, and you go out there and work by yourself? That's where they want it to go.

"We need to earn money—that's why we work, but work satisfies a certain spiritual need for us humans. I can tell you a lot of the people here have never experienced and may never experience working with a three-man switch crew. I would take working with a conductor and a switchman any day over that box. For all the reasons that you already know, it is so much better and safer. You go to work. It's a good paying job, but part of it is the social interaction. I think the work that we do on the railroad is very honorable work—the goods and the materials that we deliver. We put food on the table and TVs on people's entertainment centers.

"What little boy doesn't like trains? I remember as a kid I came down to the fishing hole and there was this little branch line that had one train a week, maybe, and when I heard this train horn and saw those guys up there, it was as if they were gods, and I thought, 'That's what I want to do.' Even though I didn't start this job until my thirties, it was always in the back of my mind. The romance is still there. I think there are some deeper needs in railroaders that get satisfied by the job that we work, and I know that for me, there are. I love what I do, hate who I work for."

CHARLIE LOFTON

Charlie Lofton, an African American man I worked with in San Jose, California, was known as "the hardest working man on the railroad." His drops were legendary.

"You need to trust me," he would say, looking right into my eyes as we prepared to drop loads uphill into a spur off the main during our brief window on Amtrak's main line.

Working with Charlie was like being on a team with an all-star quarterback. I just wanted to be good enough to work with him. Howard Halla felt the same way.

"Charlie was the foreman and we had gone to Burke Rubber and picked up a car. As we rounded the corner heading back toward the City Metals switch, Charlie ran out on the other end of the engine and pulled the pin and gave Al a little highball sign to start pulling away from the car. Without even talking about what we were going to do, everybody knew. It wasn't something we had to discuss and everybody was on the same page. Charlie got back in the engine

and it didn't take very long before we all looked at each other and without talking we all had the same sense of urgency. We realized that it probably wasn't such a hot idea to pull the pin on that car as far back as we did, going as fast as we were going, because things were only going to get worse from that point if we didn't move. Al picked up the speed quite a bit on the engine as this car was picking up speed behind us, and we widened the gap between us and the car sufficiently so that when we got down to City Metals and stopped to line the switch, we literally had just enough time to stop the engine, line the switch, get the engine in the clear, and line the switch back before the car went sailing by. If anything had gone wrong anywhere along the way, the car would have crashed right into the side of the engine. It would have been one of those 'Oh shit' moments and we would have had some explaining to do. Charlie ran for all he was worth and boarded the car, got a hand brake on it, and stopped it. We lined the switch, tied back on, and cut the air in the car without anybody saying too much and we went about our business. About halfway between where we picked the car up and Luther Junction, Charlie promised that he was going to bring extra underwear for everybody tomorrow in case we decided to do the same thing.

"What I miss most about the old railroad are those days when you were all ass and elbows and it worked, and I don't think we had nearly the number of incidents back then working the way we did than they have now with all the rules and regulations they heap upon us. It seems that every day they come up with another nitpicky thing to torment us with, and at some point we won't be able to get out the door.

"You meet a few profound people in life and Charlie was one of them. One day I was working with Charlie and we pull up to the switch and I get off the seat box to go down and throw the switch and he says, 'No, no. Wait here. You're my favorite little pickaninny. I might need you later.' And from that point on, I became HP Halla FLP (favorite little pickaninny). Then he came up with HP standing for head pickaninny. He got more miles out of that. Yeah, we miss him. The new hires won't have opportunities to work with people like that. The caliber isn't the same, and the people will never know railroads the way we did. They're not allowed to.

"I remember one time I was working with Charlie and the last move of the night was to go out and shove a car to the Butter House, and I had been sick all night, in and out of that bathroom, shitting like a trooper. I was in there sitting on the porcelain pony for about the tenth time and my radio crackles and Charlie says, 'Howard, go to beans,' which meant 'go home.' He took the car out to Lawrence and took care of that move by himself, and that's the kind of guy he was."

As good and strong as he was, though, he couldn't outrun cancer. He went into the hospital around the time of the merger and was in intensive care for months. We passed the hat and sent cards and finally we heard that he was out. He never made it back to work, but this letter appeared on the bulletin board at the Newhall yard office. I made a copy at the time and kept it with me ever since. It was a strange artifact. I was never sure where I had put it and it kept appearing and disappearing. I recently found it again, tucked into a copy of *Railroad Voices*.

Greetings to all of my fellow workers, and friends:

I hired out on the railroad in the year of April 1st, 1969. I have had the pleasure to work with many of people of different races and color. When I hired out, I was treated very well by everyone. The longer I was around, it seemed like the relationship moved from being an employee that showed up for a nine to five, to a closer relationship such as friends, and in the later years we were like family. We did the things such as a regular family does. We will get along together, protect one another (from losing our jobs etc.). We would have our arguments, and disagreements, and then we would make up and go on with life. We became concern about each other's family. Over the 30 years that I have

been with the railroad, I have a bond or affection if you will, for the guys that I work with. While you are up and in good health, people will always treat you well and say, I am your friend, if you ever need me let me know. If you want to find out if what was said is real or not, take sick and that's when you will find out who really cares about you, besides your immediate family. I am the type of person that likes to treat people, the way I would like to be treated. If I see that you are having a bad day, I will try to say something humorous to cheer you up. When I was hurt on the job, and had to go to the hospital, I will never forget the concern of my fellow workers, and the officials such as Dick Brandy and Bob Walcot. Everyone would ask me, are you alright Charlie? Will you be alright financially? When will you be able to come back? We miss you around here, etc. When I took sick and went in the hospital February 17th, 1998, seriousness of my sickness. I had what you call a bowel obstruction, which not only busted open once, but twice while I was in the hospital, two separate times. I was operated on two times, then came the complications of having pneumunia, an infection in my body, and very high fevers. These complications was enough to take my life. After my second operation, when I was in the ICU ward, not knowing who I was, where I was, or how long I was there (two months asleep), I heard a voice asking me if I wanted to live? My first reply was, that I didn't want to live long, that I wanted to live a little while longer to be with my family. The voice said that's not what I asked you. I have a job to do, let me do my job, do you want to live? My answer was yes, I wanted to live. The moment I said yes, and my mom prayed for me, everything went from a situation to improvement. Now let me tell you the part you played in my recovery. When you found out my condition, and how close to death I was, that's when you really showed your support, your concern, and your love. When I was in the ICU ward, (asleep for two months) my wife told me about how Steve Sterken tried to get in to see me. The doctors and nurses told him that only the immediate family was allowed in. Steve would not take no for an answer. He told them that he is my best friend, and he is family. The results was they let him in. I heard that Dick Young tried to get in with a get well card signed by all the guys from the job. They wouldn't let him in because the card he was caring was as big as the heart in his body. Then someone came up with the idea, let's raise a donation for him and his family. The money that you guys raised and gave to me, help out a whole lot, and I thank each and every one of you for your support, your prayers, your love, and your concern. If I would have bought a card and signed it saying thank you, it could not say what I feel in my heart. That's the reason for me writing this letter to all of you. Those of you that wasn't able to make it to the hospital to see me, sent cards, and well wishes, and some even called the hospital to see how I was progressing. A couple of people that called was, Dick Brandy, Bob Walcot, and Howard Halla who has not ceased to keep in touch, and to make sure I had some spending money in my pocket, both Howard and his lovely wife Susan. When I had arrived home from the hospital, my wife gave me a bag filled with cards and letters from all of you. I even had mail from some people that I thought had forgotten all about me. I would set down and think about what you had done for me and I would break down and cry. I am still receiving phone calls and cards. I wrote this letter to show my appreciation for how you have stuck by me. Each and every one of you have given me a reason for living. When it is my time to depart this life, I will carry each and every one of you in my heart. I can't get you into heaven, that's something we as individuals have to do ourselves. But when I come before my heavenly father, to answer for my deeds that I have done in this life, and he ask me the question **what is this that is in your heart?** *I will say these are the ones that help when I was sick and was on my death bed. Once again thank you all for what you have done for me, and may god bless you all. May you*

have a very merry Christmas, and a safe and happy new year. If it is God's will, I should be returning to work in the month of Feburary.

Love from me and my family

CHARLIE LOFTON

THE RAILROAD DROP (FOR THE NEW HIRES)

Howard and I were working the afternoon district job in the San Jose yard, looking at a reasonable quit, and we were making our last move of the night. The yardmaster had us lined into a clear rail and for 9, 11, and 13. We were dropping our head-enders into 9 rail, our middle cars into 11, and our rear-enders into 13. The yard was a dish, allowing us to drop cars easily during flat switching.

I was the pin-puller and my part of the move was to pull the pin on the engine when I got the slack, allowing it to run ahead of the rolling cars into the clear rail. Then I needed to bail off at the switch to that rail and line it down the lead, then position myself at the 9 switch to line it back for the lead once the head-enders had rolled in the clear. Howard, the field man, had dropped back to ride the cut between the head-enders and the two sets of rear-enders. The secret to getting the pin was to set a little brake, called a stinger, holding back the second set of cars to be cut off. When Howard released the brake, the slack would run in momentarily, allowing him to pull the pin, either by squatting down on the side ladder or by hooking the cut lever with the foot.

When I cut the cars off from the engine, Howard pulled the pin on the last car of the head-enders with his foot and got a little stinger on the rear-enders so that they would separate from the other cars. We now had two sets of cars rolling down the lead. As the head-enders went past me, my job was to line the switches for the lead and 11 track. When the cars rolled in the clear on 9, Howard would normally release the brake on his cars and get the next pin, then hop on the last cut of cars and get another brake. After he let those loose, he would bail off across from the yard office so he wouldn't have a long walk in. I would then let the engine out of its rail and put it away in the house.

Today, however, I panicked on lining the 9 switch back. I just wasn't sure the cars would clear in time so I left it lined for 9 and we had to get the engine out, come behind the rear-enders, hook onto them and kick some of them into 11 and the rest into 13. That took the thirty minutes we could have gone home early, the gauge by which switchmen measure their success. Howard sighed as we walked back to the yard office together.

"You know, there are just a few moments I look forward to all day," he said wistfully, "a few moments of expertise."

"I'm sorry," I said. "They probably would have cleared."

The following is Howard's recipe for the drop. He had written it out and handed it to me when we met for lunch the last time I was in Santa Cruz.

Recipe for a 6-car 3-rail drop (Newhall style)
By Howard Halla 10/13/08

Ingredients:
   1 Locomotive with engineer
   6 Railroad cars (loads—good rollers) attached to the locomotive
   4 Available rails (use TK 9, 11, 13, and House TK)
   1 Lead with sufficient grade and running room
   1 Person to handle the cars (person A)
   1 Person to operate the switches (person B)

Person B secures the line up for TK 9, 11, & 13.
Person A secures the line up for the House TK and bleeds the cars.
Person A ensures the locomotive and cars are positioned a sufficient distance from the House TK switch.

Person A positions himself on the bottom step of the locomotive on the end closest to the cars. He then gives the engineer a sign to start pulling the cars quickly in the direction of the House TK switch. When the cars have reached a speed generating sufficient momentum to ensure a successful drop, person A gives a "pin" sign to the engineer. The engineer will then back off on the throttle just enough for the slack to run in allowing person A to pull the cut lever on the locomotive separating the locomotive from the cars. Upon a successful separation, person A will give the engineer a sign to increase speed and pull away from the now free rolling cars. The locomotive will be entering the House track via the previously lined House TK switch. As the locomotive enters the House TK with the free rolling cars in hot pursuit, person A will get off of the locomotive while in motion and line the House TK switch away from the House TK and toward the receiving track lead.

Person B is positioned at the 9 TK switch as the first two cars of the six cars rolling down the lead will go into 9 TK.

Person A will pull the pin on the cars separating the first two cars from the trailing four cars. Person A will then immediately get on the third car and apply the hand brake with just enough force to allow the cars to separate, but not so much force as to kill the inertia remaining in the trailing four cars. When sufficient separation had been achieved, the hand brake on the trailing four cars is released and as their speed slowly increases, the process is repeated. The pin is pulled on the second car leaving two cars trailing, and a brake is applied on the third car as described above.

Person B, still positioned at the 9 TK switch, must determine by speed and distance the appropriate time to throw the 9 switch to allow the cars for TK 11 to proceed down the lead without striking the cars going into TK 9. Often it is a split second decision.

Person A, still positioned on the hand brake, will release the brake when sufficient separation has been achieved and the final two cars will be on their way to TK 13. At this point, if everything has gone right, the cars are where they belong, the locomotive is in the house, and we are on our way home.

The success of the above described drop is dependent upon timing, skill, and judgment. Everyone has to be on their game. If it fails, at the least it can be inconvenient. At the most, it can be a major disaster. When it is successful, it is a thing of beauty.

ABSOLUTE SIGNAL A signal that directs main line traffic, controlled by the train dispatcher.

AIR The air brake system that applies the brake shoes to the wheels when it ruptures. It consists of a compressor on the engine, brake pipes running underneath the cars, and flexible rubber hoses (called rubber), which are fastened together between the cars. When cars separate, the hoses uncouple, causing the brakes to set up.

BAD ORDER Damaged, defective.

BEANS Meal period.

BIG HOLE An emergency application of the air brakes reducing the air pressure in the brake pipe and causing the brakes to apply. Makes a distinctive sound like a giant tire being popped.

BLEED A CAR To drain the air from a car's reservoir by pulling a rod on the side of the car. Bleeding removes air brakes, but not hand brakes. It allows the car to roll freely.

BOOMER Brakeman who travels to places that are booming in order to work.

BOWL The fan-shaped tracks at the bottom of a hump, used to receive cars that are being classified. Tracks where trains are made up.

BUMP A seniority displacement.

CAR COUNTS Distance to a stop, in car lengths, given to the engineer by a trainman riding the point.

CHECK THE LIST Compare the computer printout of the cars on a track against the cars actually on the track.

CONDUCTOR Boss of the train, including the engineer.

CROSSOVERS SWITCHES Switches that allow movement from one track to another.

CSX TRANSPORTATION A railroad company.

CTC Centralized traffic control. Signal and switch system controlled by a dispatcher for authorizing main line trains.

CUT LEVER Uncoupling lever that raises the coupling pin, allowing cars to separate. Located on the side of the car.

CUT OFF To be laid off. Of cars to separate.

CUT THE CROSSING When a long train is delayed and blocks a road crossing for more than ten minutes, the cars must be separated to allow traffic to cross.

DEADHEAD Paid travel to and from an on-duty point.

DERAIL A switch that, when thrown, opens a section of rail, causing a runaway car or engine to go on the ground.

DIE ON THE LAW Work to the limit of the Federal Hours of Service Act (twelve hours).

DOG CATCHING To relieve a crew on a train that has died under the Hours of Service Act.

DOUBLE To pick up a whole track and couple it to another whole track. Of working to work two shifts in twenty-four hours.

DOUBLE RUNAROUND A complicated switching move used to switch the position of the engine on a cut of cars that won't fit into the available siding or runaround track.

D&RGW Denver & Rio Grande Western Railroad.

DRAG A slow train that isn't going anywhere fast. No priority with the dispatcher.

DRAWBAR The wrench-shaped piece of metal that the knuckle fits into. The heaviest component of a coupler and the part that remains rigid. If you break a drawbar in addition to the knuckle, you have really hit hard. Often takes two people to adjust.

DROP A skilled move used in switching to reverse the position of a car in relation to the engine. Requires teamwork. One person tends the switch; one rides on the engine ready to uncouple it in motion; a third rides the car being dropped, ready to stop it in the clear with a hand brake. The engineer starts down the track, pulling the car behind the engine. At a signal, he reduces speed momentarily, allowing the slack to run in. The pin-puller pulls the pin, uncoupling the car, and gives the engineer a highball. The engine then outraces the car to the sidetrack switch, which is thrown when the engine goes over it. The car then sails up the sidetrack and is tied down by the brakeman riding it. The engine then reverses and picks the car up from the opposite end. End of drop.

DUTCH DROP A drop in which cars are tied down by hand brakes and left on an incline. After the engine gets into a side track, the brakes are released, allowing the cars to roll past the engine, at which point they are stopped by hand brakes. The engine then comes out of the sidetrack and comes against the cars, thus reversing their relative positions.

DYNAMIC BRAKING Using the power generated by the engine's electric motors to assist in braking it.

DYNAMITER A car whose air brake system reads any reduction in air pressure as an emergency application, sending the whole train into emergency.

EARLY QUIT Going home early.

EXTRA BOARD List of available brakemen. As each brakeman is called for a job, the next in order moves up to first place (first out) to be called. The board rotates. As a brakeman reports back in from a job, he goes to the bottom of the list.

FELA Federal Employers Liability Act.

FIELD MAN Brakeman or switchman who works the position farthest from the engine. Like a center fielder.

FLAGGING Providing protection on a track by means of a person with a red flag who is there to signal to approaching trains.

FRA Federal Railroad Administration.

FRED Flashing rear end device, replacing the caboose at the end of a train and almost immediately and universally referred to as a "fucking rear end device."

FULL SERVICE APPLICATION Applying the maximum brake pipe reduction, placing the train into emergency braking.

GLADHAND Metal coupling piece on the end of an air hose. Heavy enough to break your jaw if suddenly filled with 90 pounds of pressure.

HANG Keep a hold of, as in "hang two," meaning hold on to two cars.

HEEL Hand brakes placed on cars in a track so that other cars may be kicked against them and the whole track will not roll out.

HERDER Switchman who guides engines and trains in and out of a yard, lining switches and giving them a highball with a green flag or green light.

HIGHBALL Signal meaning "Get going," or "All's well with your train."

HOGHEAD Engineer. As in the Hog Law, for Hours of Service Act.

HOTSHOT A fast freight with priority on the main line.

HUMP Man-made hill in a classification yard used to separate cars from each other by gravity. A cut of cars is shoved to the crest of the hill; the pins on several cars are pulled, and those cars roll off down the hill into one of the bowl tracks at the bottom. The process is repeated until all the cars in the cut have been separated.

IN THE CLEAR Of cars and engines: to be far enough back from the point where two tracks meet to avoid being crunched by a car on the other track. As in clearance point. Of people: to be far enough away from a track that a car rolling on that track won't hit you.

JAM Engine brakes. Separate from the train braking system.

JOINT A coupling between two cars. As in "make a joint; make a short joint," meaning the distance to the car to be coupled is short.

KICK To shove cars with force ahead of the engine so that when the engine is stopped, the cars will roll into a track on their own.

KICK SIGN Lantern sign or hand sign signaling the engineer to come ahead hard.

KNUCKLE The mobile component of a coupling device, weighing 85 pounds. Two knuckles lock together to form a joint, or couple. Knuckles are the weakest link and often shatter when a train breaks in two.

LACE THE AIR See "make the air."

LEAD Yard track from which other tracks branch off. A lead track will typically have ten other tracks leading into it in a series.

LINE BEHIND Throw a switch back after you have passed through it.

MAKE THE AIR Hook up the rubber air hoses and cut the air into them by turning the angle cock on the end of a car.

MARKER Red light at the end of a train.

MIDNIGHT GOAT Switch engine on the midnight job.

MODULES Railroad company dorms. Old head rail with a lot of seniority.

MOW Maintenance of way.

OLD HEAD Railroader with a lot of seniority.

ON THE POINT To ride on the leading end of a car or engine to protect the movement.

ON THE SPOT Time out for coffee or rest. Also to designate exact location a freight car is to be delivered to. Spotting cars in industries provides good opportunities to go on spot.

ORDER BOARD Post on which train orders are hung to be snatched up by crews on passing trains. Now obsolete.

OT Overtime.

PEE TEST Urinalysis ordered by the company.

PIGGYBACK, RAIL PACK Long light flatcar used to transport containerized freight.

PIN-PULLER Switchman who works the position closest to the engine, lining switches ahead and operating the uncoupling (cut) lever on the side of cars during switching.

POOL FREIGHT Refers to the pool of crews available in a rotating order to work on through freight trains.

PULL One of the two possible maneuvers involving an engine and cars. You either pull the cars behind the engine or shove the cars ahead of the engine. You either pull a track or shove a track.

PULL THE PIN To uncouple something. To quit the railroad, to quit anything, to die.

PUZZLE SWITCH One huge switch with four levers that will throw four sets of switch points. Used as a crossover switch between adjacent tracks. Well named.

RAIL Railroader. What the railroad runs on.

REMOTES Engines operated by a trainman or engineman on the ground using a belt pack.

ROAD FOREMAN Company official who supervises engineers.

ROLL-BY Observation of a passing train for possible defects.

ROUNDHOUSE Facility where engines are worked on. Usually round brick building with lots of windows.

RS Region/system.

RUN THROUGH A SWITCH To go through a switch without lining it for the movement, bending the switch points.

RUNAROUND Siding track used to run around cars in switching.

RWU Railroad Workers United.

SHAGGER A clerk who locates crews that are called for duty. Trainmen have the right to be called in person by a callboy if they live within a two-mile radius of their on-duty point.

SHOVE Push ahead of engine.

SLACK Amount of free motion in the coupling device between cars. Creates most of the problems in life.

SP Southern Pacific Railroad.

SPECIAL AGENT Railroad police. Bull. Spotter. Company spy.

SPUR A track that dead ends, usually in an industry.

STRETCH Order to the engineer to pull on a cut of cars to see if they are coupled up.

SWITCH LIST List of cars on a particular track and their destinations. Working instructions for a switch crew.

SYSTEM SENIORITY A seniority roster that applies on the whole territory of a railroad.

TAIL TRACK A track where switches have been lined to accommodate your movement so that you can back into this track when you're shoving cars behind the engine.

TIE 'EM DOWN Tie hand brakes on a cut of cars or engines.

TOP END One end of a yard, usually for incoming trains, but it can refer to topography.

TRAIN DISPATCHER Air traffic controller for trains. Operates power switches and signals in a specific territory. Issues train orders. Has big picture. Smokes too many cigarettes; drinks too much coffee.

TRAINMASTER Company official who is in charge of a terminal. Hides in bushes; asks questions on the book of rules. Now called manager.

TSC Total Safety Culture.

TURN To reverse the direction of a car by either running around it or dropping it. Also used for a local job that goes to a certain location and returns.

UNIT Engine.

UP Union Pacific Railroad.

UTU United Transportation Union.

VARIABLE SWITCH Switch whose points can be thrown by the wheels passing over them. The points then stay in the new direction.

WALK THE TRAIN Walk alongside the train from the rear to the head end, looking for defects.

WOBBLY Nickname for Industrial Workers of the World (IWW), an international union founded in 1905.

WORK HISTORY A computer search of how many days an employee worked in a given period. Used by the company to deter laying off.

WORK TRAIN A train that serves the maintenance-of-way department in track repair. Unloads ties, ribbon rail, and ballast.

WYE Tracks in the shape of a Y used for turning cars or engines.

YARDMASTER Person in charge of all moves within yard limits. A seniority position bid on by switchmen.

BOOKS IN THE RAILROADS PAST AND PRESENT SERIES

Landmarks on the Iron Railroad: Two Centuries of North American Railroad Engineering by William D. Middleton

South Shore: The Last Interurban (revised second edition) by William D. Middleton

Katy Northwest: The Story of a Branch Line by Don L. Hofsommer

"Yet there isn't a train I wouldn't take": Railroad Journeys by William D. Middleton

The Pennsylvania Railroad in Indiana by William J. Watt

In the Traces: Railroad Paintings of Ted Rose by Ted Rose

A Sampling of Penn Central: Southern Region on Display by Jerry Taylor

The Lake Shore Electric Railway by Herbert H. Harwood, Jr., and Robert S. Korach

The Pennsylvania Railroad at Bay: William Riley McKeen and the Terre Haute and Indianapolis Railroad by Richard T. Wallis

The Bridge at Quebec by William D. Middleton

History of the J. G. Brill Company by Debra Brill

Uncle Sam's Locomotives: The USRA and the Nation's Railroads by Eugene L. Huddleston

Metropolitan Railways: Rapid Transit in America by William D. Middleton

Perfecting the American Steam Locomotive by Parker J. Lamb

From Small Town to Downtown: A History of the Jewett Car Company, 1893–1919 by Lawrence A. Brough and James H. Graebner

Limiteds, Locals, and Expresses in Indiana by Craig Sanders

Amtrak in the Heartland by Craig Sanders

When the Steam Railroads Electrified by William D. Middleton

The GrandLuxe Express: Traveling in High Style by Karl Zimmermann

Still Standing: A Century of Urban Train Station Design by Christopher Brown

The Indiana Rail Road Company by Christopher Rund

Evolution of the American Diesel Locomotive by J. Parker Lamb

The Men Who Loved Trains: The Story of Men Who Battled Greed to Save an Ailing Industry by Rush Loving

The Train of Tomorrow by Ric Morgan

Built to Move Millions: Streetcar Building in Ohio by Craig R. Semsel

The CSX Clinchfield Route in the 21st Century by Jerry Taylor and Ray Poteat

Visionary Railroader: Jervis Langdon Jr. and the Transportation Revolution by H. Roger Grant

The New York, Westchester & Boston Railway: J. P. Morgan's Magnificent Mistake by Herbert H. Harwood, Jr.

Iron Rails in the Garden State: Tales of New Jersey Railroading by Anthony J. Bianculli

Visionary Railroader: Jervis Langdon Jr. and the Transportation Revolution by H. Roger Grant

The Duluth, South Shore & Atlantic by John Gaertner

LINDA GRANT NIEMANN teaches creative nonfiction at Kennesaw State University in Georgia. She is author of *Boomer: Railroad Memoirs* (re-titled *On the Rails*) and *Railroad Voices*.

JOEL JENSEN is a freelance photographer whose work has been featured in various publications.